Writing Handbooks

Freelance
Copywriting

Writing Handbooks

Freelance Copywriting

Diana Wimbs

A & C Black • London

First published 1999
A & C Black (Publishers) Limited
35 Bedford Row, London WC1R 4JH

© 1999 Diana Wimbs

ISBN 0–7136–4822–8

A CIP catalogue record for this book
is available from the British Library.

Typeset in 10½ on 12½ pt Sabon
Printed and bound in Great Britain by
Creative Print and Design (Wales), Ebbw Vale

Contents

For Mum and Dad

And . . .
Ron Langrish, gifted designer and good friend, who not only created the hand-drawn illustrations for this book but also advised, encouraged and supported me throughout the writing of it. Grateful thanks also to Michael Bell Limited of Lewes for their contributions and patience during my time in purdah, and to the Plain English Campaign for making it so simple to use their materials. Finally, my love and thanks to everyone at the Writers' Summer School, Swanwick, who inspired the idea for the book; to Liane, Kate and Anne for cheering me on – and, of course, to Maria and Andrew for being themselves and making me so proud of all they do and are.

Introduction

A good copywriter always looks for a fresh angle. So let's begin by turning the concept of an introduction on its head and decide what this book *isn't* about.

Bear with me, it's a more sensible opening than it sounds. Copywriters are frequently asked to explain themselves. Questions are raised about protection tactics (copyright), punctuation (copy editing) and toners (broken photocopiers). Even fellow writers are afflicted by the 'Huh?' factor and enter into earnest discussions about column widths (newspaper copy).

None of which has anything to do with copywriting but can be a great way to start – or stop – conversations.

The irony is that copywriters are employed to dispel confusion, not spread it. We use the power of words to enlighten, inform and enthuse. We're also rather good at persuading, motivating and encouraging.

Yet one of the greatest misconceptions of all is that these skills are confined to TV and press advertising alone. The truth is that copywriters are needed for an astonishing range of projects, including many that impart information or deal with sensitive and emotive issues. That's why this is such an exciting, varied and challenging field of writing. It includes letters, leaflets, flyers, brochures, posters, newsletters, press releases, questionnaires, competitions, sales aids, articles . . . the list, to coin a cliché (slap wrist), is endless.

It's hardly surprising that copywriters – especially freelances – are constantly in demand by companies and their agencies to tackle this ever-increasing Everest of work. What is surprising is that very few writers know such an opportunity exists.

And that's what this book *is* about. It clears away the clouds and reveals the facts about freelance copywriting. It also illustrates a key aspect of the art: an ability to take a subject and make it unique . . .

1

What's different about this book?

You've heard of the X-factor, that elusive quality of being rare, special and desirable? In copywriting terms, it's known as a USP – a unique selling proposition. I can think of three USPs for this book:

- Firstly, it is written by an actively employed freelance who has also worked in-house as an agency copywriter. So I speak from experience about opportunities that are right here, right now.

- Secondly, it maintains reality by concentrating on the tasks you *are* likely to tackle as a freelance, rather than straying into areas like TV advertising which is an improbable (although not impossible) opening.

- Thirdly, it not only shows you the techniques of the job – briefings, concepts, copy structure, language usage, etc – but also tells you how to *earn* from it. Such as setting fees, sending invoices, building good relationships and avoiding bad ones.

This last point brings me to the best secret of all. Freelance copywriting can be very lucrative because it is a skill that's highly valued and surprisingly scarce. Clearly, if there aren't many copywriters to the pound, people will pay more pounds for their copywriters. But that means *good* copywriters. This is a creative profession, where originality and style are as vital to your work as they are to novelists, poets and journalists. If your words don't linger on in the hearts and minds of your readers, your name won't linger long on the pay cheques of your clients.

What makes it all so compulsive?

This book adopts the same techniques as the job it describes. It starts by capturing your attention with the vast range of markets open to you and the differences between each one. Why do some copywriters work above the line and some below? How can you follow it through? What's the right – and wrong – way to approach agencies and businesses, start a portfolio and make your name known?

As your interest builds, so does the momentum. Discover the secrets behind the art (and science) of persuasion. Why are children so good at it? How can you avoid woolly briefs? Or translate ticklish ones? For instance, do you know the difference between an advertorial and an advertisement? A bangtail and billing stuffer? Landscape and portrait? Gate fold and roll fold? There's an entire chapter devoted to technicalities like these, complete with illustrations.

Desire beginning to mount? The fires are stoked by taking you behind the scenes at a typical agency briefing meeting. Learn how the thinking process starts and creativity is born. Draw the parallels between copywriting and other writing genres: drama, conflict, colourful characters, tantalising suspense. How can you put a new slant on old clichés? Put paid to puns? Attract with opposites? Take the right point of view? The pace continues with the latest word on style, tips for structuring and revising your copy, resisting ticklers and taking criticism on the chin. All with the help of practical working examples.

Ready to take action? Wait, there's another market to explore: the art of writing 'Plain English'. Why did the NHS use 160 words to describe a hospital bed? When does a traffic jam become a localised capacity deficiency, and what turns pigs, sheep and cows into grain-consuming units? We move on to the business end of freelancing, with practical advice on everything from sorting out your fees to handling orders and invoices.

And just in case you are still hesitating, there's a further call to action at the end with a sample campaign to inspire your launch onto the local business scene.

If you love words, prefer fact to fiction and can spot a spelling mistake at fifty paces, this book is for you. And since it began by blowing away the clouds of confusion surrounding copywriting, here's a silver lining.

Just think – in such a little-known profession, the opportunities to shine are endless!

1. Great Openings

There's nothing like encouragement to fire the imagination. So let me start by saying there's a huge market for copywriters and surprisingly few people are filling it.

Why?

Because many writers and would-be writers simply don't know such a market exists.

Copywriters have much the same attributes as any other writers: a love of words, a sense of imagination, a respect for deadlines and an affection for their readers. Apart from that, there's nothing 'typical' about copywriters. They come in male and female form, in various ages and sizes. Some have impressive literary, arts or business degrees, while many more do not. There are those who prefer writing about familiar subjects and others who enjoy the challenge of breaking new ground.

If there is a common denominator, it's a tendency to ask questions. As Chapter 3 (and others) will illustrate, persuasion may be an art but its palette is strictly scientific.

I mentioned earlier that copywriters have an affection for their readers. With that in mind, I'd like to get to know you before we go on, so that this book is as helpful and relevant as possible.

- Are you a published writer or journalist who wants to explore new outlets (and earning opportunities) for your talents?
- Do you teach others to write, or edit other writers' work, and long to write for yourself?
- Are you suffering the frustrations of trying to get your first writing break and haven't yet found your forte?
- Do you work in an agency or business environment and want some tips on how the creative side of things is run?

- Or are you just fed up with the job you're in and desperate to try something different?

If you are wondering how I know the kind of work you do and the ambitions you cherish, it's because I've made it my job to find out. You are my target audience and I'd be a pretty poor copywriter if I tried to sell you on the subject of this book without knowing anything about you.

Writing to inform

Would it surprise you to know that the Government may offer some of the best openings for copywriters in the country? Think about all those leaflets and posters in Job Centres, post offices, hospitals and DSS offices. They were all written by professionals to help people make sense of the baffling or bewildering.

I'm not suggesting you drop a line to No. 10 offering your services (although it never hurts to try). But if you are good at turning relatively complex information into clear, simple English, this is an area of copywriting that's very much in demand.

So, too, is the ability to 'translate' legal and technical documents into everyday language. It takes skill and patience to tackle jobs like these, as the translation must be legally watertight to protect both the business and its customers. But many organisations find it more cost-effective to start the process with a copywriter than to have senior legal people tied up for days, rewriting official documents from scratch. Chapter 8 explores this growing market in greater depth.

Writing to advise

If you have ever suffered a traumatic experience, or been worried about a risk to your health or safety, the chances are that you read something at the time which put your mind at rest, or at least pointed you in the right direction for help. And there's an equally good chance that it was written by a copywriter.

It might be a leaflet explaining how a particular counselling or therapy service works. Or an information sheet encouraging you to take better care of your health. It might even be a poster in an airport, railway station or bus terminus alerting you to potential travel dangers.

5

The more sensitive or emotive the subject, the more likely it is that a professional writer has been used to put the message across. By way of example, my copy portfolio currently includes literature on funeral planning, stress counselling, diabetes health management and women's pension rights.

Writing to sell

I've left this section until last for the simple reason that it covers the biggest market for copywriters. We are, primarily, employed to sell things to people. Agencies and their clients prefer to call it 'marketing', but it boils down to the same thing. A well-written advertisement, leaflet or brochure is an essential part of the seduction of your hearts and wallets.

Some copywriters focus on specialised areas such as food, finance, science or health, while others deal with a much wider spectrum. Most can turn their hands (and computers) to almost anything, given the right information.

Drawing the line: how copywriting tasks are classified

When an organisation launches a new product or service, or wants to raise awareness of an existing one, its first task is to decide how much money can be spent on the campaign. Once a budget has been agreed, the next step is to decide how the campaign should be run in order to achieve its aims. In advertising and marketing terms, campaigns are usually divided into three categories:

- **'Above the line'**: high-impact media and poster advertising
- **'Below the line'**: marketing, sales promotions and PR
- **'Through the line'**: a bit of both

This is a simplified description of a fairly complex mix, but it serves to explain why some copywriters have 'advertising' before their names and others do not.

Advertising copywriters specialise in turning clients into household names and household names into clients. Some of them work for days with storyboards, art directors, TV producers and camera crews to create something that lasts seconds on screen, yet can earn them a fee with almost as many digits as the number of words they use.

I'm exaggerating, of course, with more than a hint of envy in my voice. However, I am quite serious in saying that above-the-line copywriting is a tougher area to break into. Most advertising agencies employ talented young teams of writers and designers who have an impressive range of qualifications for the job. But it's also true to say that agency bosses are always on the look-out for fresh talent, so if this is an area that appeals to you, it is certainly worth a try.

Although I've tried to make this book as wide-ranging as possible, I need to 'draw the line' myself to do justice to the topics it covers. As TV advertising is such a specialised area, I've decided against including it. However, many of the techniques involved are no different from those you will discover over the coming chapters.

Maximising your potential

The best way to ensure a steady flow of work is to write 'through the line'. Thousands of agencies make their living by either producing the materials needed to support TV, press and poster campaigns, or by creating alternative strategies. And all these agencies need copywriters to tackle the work.

Let's start by exploring the opportunities in general, then take a closer look at individual aspects.

This little piggy went to market

Take a leg of pork. You might think that copywriting has little to do with your Sunday crackling, but you'd be surprised. When you peruse all those joints in your local supermarket, look for a leaflet dispenser alongside. A copywriter has been hard at work to reassure you that your cut was lovingly raised, humanely felled and hygienically packed.

If you see a cardboard butcher enticing you to 'Pick up a piece of pork, Percy,' a copywriter's had a hand in it (so to speak). Behind the scenes, that same copywriter has probably written newsletters, press releases, brochures, articles and a host of other practical pieces on pork — and been paid handsomely for doing so.

7

But before you rush off to the nearest pig farm to offer your services, it's worth taking a look at the other options available.

Copywriters everywhere . . .

Ever read a cornflakes packet? A copywriter was behind all that sunshine and goodness. Looked inside your Sunday paper? That deluge of leaflets was written by someone (guess who?) Hooked on competitions? A copywriter persuaded you to buy the product you needed to enter – and probably devised the competition as well.

May I advise a note of caution on this last point. A food company once asked me to create a word-search competition to promote the versatility of eggs. I had a whale of a time sneaking in 'scrambled', 'fried', 'omelette' etc, before surrounding the words with random letters. Just before sending it off for publication, I tried it out on some colleagues.

'You should be able to find ten words,' I told them. They retreated to a corner, pens in hand. Muffled sniggers arose, followed by roars of laughter. I began to suspect that something was amiss.

'We found an eleventh word,' they said. Horrified, I saw the biological name for a gentleman's most treasured feature triumphantly circled between 'boiled' and 'poached'.

People of letters

Many people acquire copywriting skills at a very early age. Think back to all those hand-knitted sweaters from Aunt Gladys. How long did it take you to compose a suitably appreciative letter?

Copywriters can earn a very comfortable living by writing letters. Thousands of pounds' worth go into recycling bins every day. Some of them even get read. The next time you receive a *Reader's Digest* mailing, take their 'win it, don't bin it' slogan to heart. A copywriter spent hours writing all that stuff, so read it, learn from it, *then* bin it.

Impressed by the warmth and sincerity of your insurance company when renewal time comes around again? Or the heartfelt plea of charities that your money really does make a difference? Of course it does, but it takes a skilled professional to make you sit up and take notice.

People of literature

One of the biggest markets for copywriters is business literature. Every company needs to promote itself, since modesty plays little part in the corporate success ladder. At the very least, businesses need brochures to describe themselves, their products and their philosophy in life. Best of all, they will need to update this literature on a regular basis as new products and services are introduced or customer perceptions change. It can keep copywriters occupied for years.

Take, for example, a car manufacturer. Among other things, it will need a brochure about the company, one for each model, a leaflet about the guarantee and a 'how to' guide for the stereo. And that's not counting all the mailshots about new registrations and special offers that drop through your letterbox at regular intervals. The same company may also want literature, posters and other motivational pieces for its staff, dealer network and the people who supply the parts. An enterprising copywriter can usually suggest a whole range of other bits as well.

People in the news

If you have a streak (or more) of the journalist in you, press releases and newsletters are another big market for copywriters.

All companies, even small local businesses, like to stay in the news and will welcome the chance of editorial coverage, especially if they spend large sums on press advertising. Many also like to put out regular newsletters to their customers and staff, but do not have the time or skills to tackle the job themselves.

If you can put up a convincing argument to companies or their PR agencies of your talent in this area — perhaps by sending them a press release or newsletter about yourself — you could be kept blissfully busy for months, if not years.

People of few words

We've already touched on the skills of advertising copywriters. Even if you don't get the chance to hear your words on TV or see them in the national press, you could easily be asked to write other types of advertisements.

This is where your ability to 'write tight' is put to the ultimate test. We will look at the different techniques later, but it's worth mentioning now that the more you put in an ad, the less likely it is to be read. Even the most eye-catching headline will fail to captivate your audience if they're faced with *War and Peace* below it. And your hardest task will be to convince clients of this simple but essential fact.

Getting down to business

If your whistle is now well and truly whetted, here's something else you will like about copywriting. It has the potential to earn you a very good living, usually in the comfort of your own home with the cat purring contentedly behind you – or is that you I can hear?

I'm not saying copywriting is easy. What I *am* saying is that I know from experience (and many working nights) that the demand for good copywriters is enormous. Why else would I have the courage to write this book? There's a particular demand for freelance copywriters, especially from agencies who either do not want, or cannot afford, the commitment of putting you on the payroll. Using freelances offers them greater flexibility to fit the writer to the job with none of the responsibility of sick pay, pensions and holidays.

That brings me to the only real drawback of working on a freelance basis. Many writers already work this way, but if you are used to a regular salary, with all the reassurance of permanent employment, the freelance route offers considerably less security. There's no guarantee of a regular flow of work, and no money coming in if you're ill or need a holiday.

On the plus side, you will have more freedom to boost your earnings by working freelance, so it's easier to save for rainy days. In fact, you'll have more freedom full stop. You can work the hours that suit you rather than an employer, provided you meet agreed deadlines. And by building relationships with clients on your own terms, you can become a valued member of the team without having to get involved in office politics or power struggles.

I've worked on both an employed and freelance basis and have a strong preference for the latter. It offers greater variety in my working life and, because I have built good relationships with the agencies and companies for whom I write, there is a degree of security. Once you've proved your worth your skills will be valued, especially if you have a particular talent in one area or another.

But job security (or lack of it) is an important point to consider when weighing up the pros and cons of working freelance.

2. First Steps

Writers tend to be a practical bunch of people. So it isn't surprising that most of the writers I meet want to know the 'how' of getting into freelance copywriting before asking the 'what' of doing the job.

It's a logical line of enquiry, since there's little point in pursuing opportunities that are limited to the gifted few or the comfortably bankrolled. This chapter will, I hope, demonstrate that everyone with the determination to try has an equal chance of success (although an element of luck never does any harm).

I got my first break by going to work on an egg. Not, sadly, by writing that famous slogan (it was penned by Fay Weldon), but by joining the publicity arm of the Eggs Authority when quangos were in fashion. When they went out of fashion, I started freelancing for a local agency whose client list included a major egg producer (corporate, not feathered). For months I wrote about eggs in education, eggs in catering, eggs in supermarkets: the opportunities were eggless. In due course, I persuaded the agency director that I could be trusted with other subjects and was given a leaflet to write for a firm of accountants. I knew nothing about accountancy, but I had learned to smile winningly and ask the right questions. Now I write for airlines, banks, health insurers, housing developers and anyone else who wants to pay me large sums for doing something I love for a living.

And so can you.

Learning by example

The best starting point for (a) increasing your understanding of what the job involves and (b) deciding whether you really want to do it, is to read what other copywriters write. There is no cost involved and no shortage of research materials. Dozens of examples land on your doormat every week, or leap out at you from papers and magazines. Some are beautifully written and designed, others are less so. The important thing is to read everything, learn from the good examples and be critical of the poor ones.

Ask yourself what makes one advertisement more successful than another. Could you do better? Does this leaflet have greater impact than that – and if so, why? Are you more gripped by the sales message of one company than that of its competitors? Or impressed by the letter they have sent inviting your custom? Is there too little information to go on, or too much to take in?

More specifically, which area of the job appeals to you most? Are you a headline thinker or sales copy wordsmith? Do you find yourself mentally re-creating press advertisements, or is a poorly worded letter or leaflet a greater challenge? Could you have thought up that terrific sales gimmick that popped through your letterbox, or the clever message on the envelope encasing it? Are you drawn to materials of a more factual or explanatory nature than those which promote the product or service?

Don't misunderstand me. Copywriters – especially freelances – can be required to write any and all of these. But you will feel more confident about approaching potential clients if you know what is expected of you and can promote your strengths with honesty and enthusiasm.

Catch-22 – the portfolio

There is one hurdle you will need to overcome when starting out as a freelance copywriter. Potential clients – especially agencies – may ask to see your portfolio. It's the catch-22 of the advertising and marketing world. Fresh talent is always in demand, but only if you can show evidence that your talent exists . . .

Let's start with the practicalities. In terms of appearance, portfolios can range from handsome leather-bound creations to a plastic bag. The latter may sound a little casual, but remember that the person you are seeing is more interested in what you have written than how expensively it is packaged. If you have to fumble with a folder to get at the piece they want to read, you risk losing both their interest and their patience.

13

Now for the tricky bit. What can you put inside your portfolio? If you have had anything published – even a letter in the newspaper – this is an obvious starting point. Your target audience will be impressed that you have appeared in print and can assess your writing style from the examples you give. Authorship of books or articles will impress them even more, especially agencies. Few could resist the opportunity of telling their clients that they have a published writer on their copywriting team.

Whatever you decide to use, never be tempted to pass another copywriter's work off as your own. It's not so much a question of honesty as a matter of survival. Imagine this as a scenario:

'Hello Mr. Creative Director. I see you handle the account for Safari Adventures in Swaziland. I've written extensive copy for similar ventures and would like to join your copywriting team.'

'Sounds interesting. Let's see your portfolio.' (*Studied silence for some minutes.*) 'Well, the good news is I like your style. The bad news is it's *my* style. Now show me something original . . .' (*Exit copywriter.*)

Even if you get away with showing work that is not your own, you are entering dangerous territory. You have to keep up the pretence, which could either land you in hot water when your copy fails to live up to the standard of the one you've 'stolen', or place you in the embarrassing position of having to answer questions on something you know little or nothing about.

If you really want to illustrate your potential as a copywriter, try writing something aimed at the agency or company you are approaching. Ask them about their client list or product range (they will usually give you this information over the phone if you explain why you want it), then work on a sample press advertisement or leaflet to demonstrate your writing skills. If possible, try and pick up any current literature or advertising materials they have produced to show you've done your homework. You might be able to spot a new angle that will impress them with your ability to think creatively.

To give you a more concrete example, suppose you see an ad for XYZ Advertising and Marketing Consultants in Yellow

Pages or on the Internet which tells you they specialise in working for clients in the travel industry. Gather together as many travel-related advertisements, leaflets, brochures and other materials as possible, read them carefully, then use the information – and the tips in this book – to write something that could help the agency attract new clients and, more importantly, attract them to your services.

Take your time, remember to use the spell-checker on your computer, then leave the copy to marinate in a stiff gin and tonic overnight. If it still reads well in the morning, you have a valuable item for your portfolio when contacting XYZ.

Try not to get too disheartened if your first attempts fail to attract a response. Just remind yourself that many best-selling writers suffer rejections at the start, but perseverance pays off (usually).

Familiarity breeds content

Writing about what you know is as good a way to get started in copywriting as it is in any other kind of writing. You will certainly feel more confident about approaching potential clients if you know something about the type of business they handle.

For instance, if you're a keen gardener, some of the garden centres in your area might welcome an offer to write a sales leaflet or press release for them. The same goes for service providers in other 'hobby' areas: golf courses or leisure centres for example. But do spend a bit of time visiting each outlet first so that you know as much as possible about the services each one provides, the customers it attracts and the way it is currently promoting itself.

A friend landed a useful job recently by doing just that. He visited an expensive local gym which, despite the quality of its facilities and the prestigious nature of its surroundings, had nothing better than a badly printed black and white price list to hand out to prospective members. Being a designer, he took the initiative and created a colourful leaflet which focused as much on the benefits of joining the gym as on the price of membership. The owners were so impressed that they had the leaflet printed immediately and paid him well for his input.

The great thing about approaching small or independent businesses is that they often write their own literature, which takes up valuable time and effort. So they could be delighted to find a local copywriter who understands how they operate. Even if they employ agencies to do the work, they might welcome the chance to 'buy direct' from you and save themselves some money.

Don't be fooled into thinking it is easier to break into the small business market. They tend to operate on much tighter budgets and will want some pretty tough arguments – or hard evidence as my friend's example shows – to convince them of your value.

Cultivating your own company

If you are not already a full-time writer, it could be worth exploring the opportunities for freelance copywriting within your present job, or with companies for whom you have worked in the past.

- **In-house journals**: does the company produce a staff newsletter? If so, get scribbling. There's every chance they will welcome a contribution and you can build some useful pieces for your portfolio. If you are in daily contact with customers, keep a note of any (repeatable) comments or feedback you receive. The same goes for colleagues. Whether they are delighted, disgruntled or dismayed, you can turn a useful piece of inside information into a hard-hitting article or letter. And, since most in-house newsletters are internally produced, you could make a harassed staff editor very happy indeed.

- **Marketing departments**: if you work (or used to work) for a relatively large company, the chances are that they handle some of their publicity and marketing materials in-house. I say 'some', because most large companies employ outside agencies to handle the more sophisticated stuff – press and TV ads, direct mail and so forth. If your company does have an in-house marketing department, they could be very interested to hear from you. Make an appointment to see the marketing director or manager and sell yourself for all you are worth. Remember, a writer who knows the subject as well as you do – *and* saves on outside agency costs – is likely to be good news.

- **Associated advertising and PR agencies:** if you can't see any blossoming opportunities within the company itself, an approach to one of its agencies could bear fruit. Again, you have valuable inside knowledge that they can turn to their advantage and you can turn to yours. If you draw a blank, it might be worth trying other agencies with a similar client list. You still have the power to attract them through your specialist experience, and they won't be averse to a little inside information about the opposition. The simplest way to find out which agencies a company uses is to phone and ask. Few will object to giving you this information – and they might even give you a contact name and number as well.

How to present yourself

You may want to invest in printed notepaper and business cards to impress potential clients. If so, what do you call yourself?

The obvious solution is to use your own name plus any impressive qualifications you can attach to it – 'published author' or 'journalist and business writer', for example. I prefer this route as it has an air of professionalism, although I confess to being biased. When I first set up as a freelance copywriter, I spent hours poring over the dictionary and thesaurus before coming up with the brilliant acronym of 'CAPS' (Copywriting and Publicity Services). So impressed was I by my cleverness that I had letterheads and business cards printed, not to mention expensive ads in the business media and Yellow Pages.

Over the next few months, I received more than a few phone calls and faxes offering me everything from sponsorship to printing services. Other companies were, you see, assuming that I was in the business of producing sporty hats. The final indignity came when I was sent a magazine of the top-shelf variety with a covering letter inviting me to take advertising space. When my colour had returned to a more normal hue, I rang the publishers in some indignation, demanding an explanation.

It transpired that they had put an entirely different interpretation on 'CAPS', at which point I admitted defeat and changed all my business literature into my own name.

If you do decide to adopt this route, you may find it useful to make some distinction in terms of your bank account. Having

17

personal and business accounts in the same name can cause confusion, although it is relatively simple to add 'Freelance copywriter', or even 'trading as' for the benefit of the bank, Inland Revenue, VAT office and your accountant.

Making your name known

Once you've decided what to call yourself, the next step is to make as many people aware of your name as possible.

If you have access to the Internet, it could be worth investing in your own website. Many of the agencies and businesses you approach are likely to promote themselves this way and may expect the same of you. Some of the more traditional advertising routes – Yellow Pages, for example – can be disappointing. I always received more calls from sellers of faxes and photocopiers than I ever did from potential new clients. A more productive route could be to try the specialist business media read by your target audience. Leading publications in the agency world are:

- *Campaign*: a Haymarket business publication covering agency and business news, interviews, media information, new advertising campaigns and job vacancies. For subscription details call (020) 8845 8545 or fax (020) 8845 7696. For advertising and editorial call (020) 7413 4588 and (020) 7413 4036 respectively. Email address: campaign@haynet.com.

- *Marketing*: another Haymarket publication which, as its name implies, focuses more on the marketing industry. Covers market research, industry news, interviews and job vacancies. Website address: http://www.marketing.haynet.com, otherwise same contact numbers and postal address as *Campaign*.

- *Marketing Week*: smaller in size but long-established and packed with news and articles. It has a dedicated *Creative Resources* advertising section, although the copy I have features photo-libraries and nothing else. The number to call for this section is 020 7970 6342, otherwise you can call them for further information on 020 7970 4000, or visit their website on http://www.marketing-week.co.uk.

- *Precision Marketing*: a marginally less expensive but well produced weekly which focuses mainly on the 'direct' side of the business (direct mail packs, direct marketing campaigns, etc). Includes a 'review of the week' section which looks at a selection of recently produced campaigns and names the art directors and copywriters responsible (a useful platform if you appear among them, as I have). For further information, their main switchboard number is (020) 7970 6666 and their email address is precision-marketing@centaur.co.uk.

- *Design Week*: probably of greater value to designers than writers, but an interesting and respected publication nonetheless. Same main switchboard number as *Precision Marketing* plus a complicated array of email addresses which would take up the rest of the chapter to list.

Advertising space in all these publications is likely to be expensive, so check them out first to see if they offer the best platform for you. Some of the larger libraries may have copies but if not, you will find them on sale in WH Smith and other main newsagents.

If you are more interested in targeting local businesses, you should be able to get free copies of local business magazines. My area – Sussex – is covered by *South East Business* and *Sussex Business News* which arrive on my doorstep every month. Alternatively, you could research the trade magazines and newspapers which deal specifically with the business areas you would like to target. *Willings Press Guide* and *Benn's Media* are two of the best reference sources and should be available in your local library.

Frankly, I believe that the best – and cheapest – way to make yourself known is by personal contact. You have the writing and communication skills, so use them to your advantage in letters and telephone calls. Even if companies and agencies are not looking for freelance copywriters at the time, they will usually keep interesting approaches on file for future reference. I have received approaches (and commissioned projects) from clients as much as 18 months after contacting them. And all it cost me was the price of a first class stamp.

Talking to the right people

There's a good chance that, even if you make initial contact with an agency or company by phone, they will ask you to write in and tell them about yourself. If so, you need the right information before you start – just as you will when writing copy.

To give your letter the best possible chance, find out the name of the person you should be writing to. This might sound rather obvious, but you will save several trees and at least one therapy session by sending your carefully crafted masterpiece to someone who wants to read it. A would-be copywriter once sent me a letter addressed to 'The Head Honcho'. As I work alone (not counting two cats and an optimistic blackbird), the title was technically accurate, but wildly inappropriate. Being a decent sort, I opened it anyway. Unfortunately, the author went from bad to worse by telling me that my 'creative team' (two of whom were trying to eat the third at the time) needed his unique style to add an edge to theirs. The blackbird wasn't convinced and neither was I.

A poorly researched business letter is a waste of time and postage for anyone. For copywriters it's the kiss of death. Because if we can't be bothered to target our own letters properly, how can we convince clients that we will do any better with theirs?

Always telephone first to ask who deals with your sort of enquiry. Check the spelling of their name and make a note of their job title. If the person who answers the phone shows an interest, keep talking. They could be the deciding influence about which letters 'go through' to the boss and which don't. This initial call can also be useful in finding out:

- what sort of products/services/clients they handle
- whether they write their own materials
- what agencies they use or companies they represent
- their views on using freelances

A busy reception desk may offer to put you through to someone else rather than clog the lines while answering your questions. That's great, because now you can drop another name into your letter to show you have taken the time and trouble to check your facts.

Remember that you are writing to busy people, so keep the letter short, friendly and to the point. Add any relevant experience, qualifications or writing accolades on a separate sheet of paper so they can find the information they want quickly and easily.

Once the letter has been sent, don't expect them to beat a path to your door. They are unlikely to do so. Wait for two or three days, then make a follow-up telephone call. If they are interested, they will suggest a meeting. If not, you will get to know the receptionist's voice very well. That's the time to cast your net on fresh waters, or at least look for some easier fishing grounds.

Sample Letter of Introduction (Agencies)

Dear [senior contact name]

I hear you are looking for talent . . .

It was good talking to [first contact name] today, especially as I understand you are keen to explore new copywriting skills to match the challenging and exciting growth in your client list.

Could we get together to discuss the opportunities? I am enclosing a brief outline of my writing qualifications and experience, although I would much prefer to show you actual examples. In fact, I was so inspired by seeing [famous company name] on your Website client list that I have written a sample [ad] [sales leaflet] [press release] which offers a new slant on their current [advertising] [marketing] strategy.

Please give me a call any time, or email me on [mailbox address]. I'll be delighted to come in and see you at a time to suit – evenings, if you prefer. I know the pressure deadlines can bring during the day.

Kind regards,

Jane Smith

This is, perforce, a fairly basic example of the kind of letter you might send. Obviously, you need to tailor it to emphasise your specific writing skills and experience, but it should give you a working basis from which to start. We will be exploring ways of launching you on the freelance market in terms of local businesses in Chapter 10.

Who's who and what's what?

Knowing the name of the person you are speaking or writing to is one thing. But it will also be helpful to understand the role they play in the organisation, if only to save yourself from going all out to impress someone who then refers you on to somebody else.

Of course, this might happen anyway but at least you can pace yourself as you pass along the pecking order.

The following is a short-list of key people and their roles in business and agency life. I can only give you my understanding of who's who and what's what, based on personal working relationships over the years. Some of the job titles will change from business to business, but the following should serve as a rough guide to help you know who you are dealing with and the influence they are likely to have over any future relationship together.

- **Creative Director:** this is the person you most need to impress when approaching an agency. The Creative Director generally has the final say in deciding whether to use you or not, largely because he or she is also responsible for the quality of copy-writing and design that the agency produces for its clients. Larger agencies often assign individual Creative Directors to specific projects, while others share the role between their top designer and copywriter.

- **Art Director/Designer:** this is the gifted person most likely to be your opposite number in agency circles and the one who has the skills to breathe life into every word you write. He or she will work closely with you in creating a visual link between words and imagery, from positioning headlines and pictures on the page to masterminding a photographic shoot.

- **Marketing Director:** more likely to feature in larger organisations, this is another influential person from your perspective. Marketing Directors not only oversee existing promotional methods but are also responsible for analysing changing trends and assessing the buying habits of customers. This means that they are actively involved in the creative output of the organisation or agency in terms of ensuring that it is relevant, hard-hitting and customer-focused.

- **Account Director (aka Client Services Director/New Business Director):** principally found in agencies, this role is either filled by one senior person or a team of people (depending on the size and structure of the agency). Job responsibilities revolve around spearheading existing client accounts and seeking new ones. These people tend to command considerable respect from clients because it is their responsibility to service the account, keep tabs on the market and develop a mutually productive working relationship.

- **Account Manager/Account Executive:** one of a band of hard-working agency people who are responsible for co-ordinating client projects from initial brief to printed item. They have less influence over whether your talents are used by the agency or not – but are extremely important to you in terms of keeping the jobs rolling in when you have made your mark. Get to know them as soon as you possibly can.

- **Financial Director:** likely to feature in both companies and agencies, this is someone you should take out for a drink on a regular basis. The Financial Director is the person who agrees your invoices and passes your cheque for payment each month. He or she may also be the person who decides whether the organisation can afford to use your services in the first place. Cultivate their respect at all costs.

- **Administrative/Accounts Assistants:** lower down the pecking order than the Financial Director but just as essential for your professional well-being. These are the lovely and much-needed individuals who take your phonecalls, pass on messages, put you in touch with the people who count and tackle the practical side of your relationship with the agency or company concerned – i.e. writing out and posting your cheque each month. Absolute jewels.

Practical steps when starting out

Many of you may already be in the writing business, in which case you need no advice from me about setting up a home office.

Even if you are not, I won't attempt to talk technology with you. Apart from the fact that I know little more about it than the perfunctory knowledge necessary to operate my computer, software and modem, everything changes at such terrifying speeds that I would have to update this book every two or three weeks to keep up.

What might be more helpful are a few tips on organising your workload and some of the essentials I live and work by. Note the personal pronoun: your preferences and priorities could be quite different from mine.

Keeping the paperwork under control

If you have vast quantities of space – and money – to house endless filing cabinets filled with past and present jobs, interesting reference materials, book-keeping essentials and other miscellany, so much to the good.

If not, you may prefer to adopt a system of envelopes, document wallets and boxes, as I do.

Beneath my desk is a box of large sturdy envelopes which serve as 'job bags' for every new task I am briefed to tackle. Each is labelled with the title of the project, a job number (if provided) and a list of contents.

I then file everything pertaining to the job inside the envelope, from initial brief to accompanying notes, faxes and reference materials. When the job is done, I sort through the envelope for anything worth keeping (other than the copy itself, which is stored on computer disk), then ditch it to make space for the next job.

Much the same method is applied to my VAT and book-keeping records. The only difference is that I use smaller envelopes and hang on to the contents for longer.

Building a reference library

This is a matter of such personal preference that I hesitate to include it all. However, as I'm asked regularly which reference books I use, here goes.

Being a 'dictionaholic', I have an insatiable desire for dictionaries and other word-related reference sources. As I am also an incurable optimist, you won't be surprised to learn that many of the examples on my bookshelves emanate from *Reader's Digest* (as they say, you have to be in it to win it). Some of the following may now be out of print, but they could be worth seeking out in boot sales and other sources.

- *Reader's Digest Oxford Complete Wordfinder*: I love this book. It combines a first-rate dictionary, basic thesaurus and numerous appendices on everything from punctuation marks to proverbs. An expensive outlay at the time (1993) but worth every penny.

- *Reader's Digest Great Illustrated Dictionary in two volumes*: if I can't find the word I need elsewhere, this is the source I turn to. As the title indicates, there is twice the scope to research the meaning, origin and usage of words, coupled with colourful illustrations and associated historical, geographical and biographical details. An expensive outlay initially but well worth it over the years.

- *The Oxford Illustrated Dictionary*: perhaps I'm just a pictures gal, but this is another old friend I'd hate to lose to that final boot sale in the sky. It combines both a dictionary and encyclopaedia in one volume.

- *The Oxford Dictionary for Writers and Editors*: having seen this recommended in other books for writers, I spotted a volume in my local charity shop and snapped it up. An invaluable reference source for vocabulary and usage.

- *The Cassell Concise English Dictionary*: what can I say? I love dictionaries and this completes any gaps in others that I own.

- *Chambers English Super-Mini Dictionary*: ditto, especially if I am working away from home and need a bite-sized reference source to fit into my briefcase.

- *The Right Word at the Right Time*: another *Reader's Digest* publication which failed to win me a fortune but has otherwise proved a good friend over the years. It sets out the rights and wrongs of English language usage in a clear, readable format which – in my view – puts classics like Partridge's *Usage and Abusage* in the shade.

- *Bloomsbury Thematic Dictionary of Quotations*: when I'm not being a dictionaholic, I am a confessed quotaholic (as you can see from the next few entries). This is a vintage example of quotable quotes, referenced by theme, author and opening line.

- *The Penguin Dictionary of Modern Humorous Quotations*: a cheeky little number, also thematically referenced, which can give you or your copy a lift (always remembering the 70-year copyright law, of course).

- *The Penguin Dictionary of Quotations*: slightly more formal than its humorous counterpart but an invaluable addition to the bookshelf nevertheless.

- *The Cassell Dictionary of Appropriate Adjectives*: lists around 4000 nouns with corresponding adjectives. Invaluable if you have used the same one twice and need to find a quick alternative.

- *Dictionary of Clichés* (James Rogers): a book I have owned, treasured and used for years. Lists over 2000 examples, complete with explanations of how they originated.

- *Penguin Dictionary of English Idioms*: a useful companion to the above (although I am still trying to work out the difference between an idiom and a cliché).

- *Roget's Thesaurus of English Words and Phrases*: need I say more?

- *Penguin Dictionary of English Synonyms and Antonyms*: having ordered this to slake my addiction, I found it a little disappointing and still tend to use Roget as the preferred option.

3. The Art (and Science) of Persuasion

How do you persuade people you have never met to stop what they are doing, take note of what you say and act on your suggestions?

By giving them a very good reason to do so.

This might seem blindingly obvious, but many would-be copywriters start out with the notion that the job is all about manipulating words into clever combinations. Then they discover what the rest of us have learnt the hard way. It's not the cleverness of your words that counts. It's the cleverness of your arguments.

Does it stack up?

Say, for example, I asked you to take a running jump. It might startle you a bit, given the warm and friendly nature of my advice so far, but would you be intrigued? Or would the book take an athletic leap into the bin?

How about if I accompanied the request with pictures of parachutists or bungee jumpers? Obviously, it takes on quite a different meaning – but would it capture your attention? Or even your interest? What on earth (to coin a phrase) does any of this have to do with a book about copywriting?

Quite so.

No matter how cleverly the words and pictures work together, they lack credibility because they are meaningless to their audience. But if I changed the message to '*What makes copywriters take a running jump?*' and supported it with scientific evidence that aerial gymnastics can radically improve your career prospects, would I have your attention?

Happily, this preposterous suggestion has no basis in fact whatsoever. But it does illustrate a fundamental principle of the copywriter's art. First make sure of your facts, *then* find a persuasive way to put them across. This book, for instance, was inspired by other writers asking me how, when and why I do my job. Yet that alone would not have persuaded an editor to invest time and money in publishing it. I had to produce hard evidence that such a book was needed, there was an audience for it and that I had the necessary skills and experience to write it.

Exactly the same principle applies to the launch of a new business, product or service – and to your success in persuading people to take it seriously.

As every child knows

In essence, advertising and marketing is all about knowing the strengths of your subject and the weaknesses of your audience. If you want to see a master at work, watch a child campaigning for something loud and expensive in the run-up to Christmas.

Admittedly, you may be less well versed in the educational benefits of the latest games console than the average 12-year old – or the psychological profile of his/her parents during the festive season – but you can guarantee a thorough briefing on both if that is the objective of your task.

Gathering the facts

All sensible writers research their subject first and copywriters are no exception. However, we do have one supreme advantage: most of the information we need is handed to us on a plate. The fact is that clients *want* us to do a good job for them, because they are paying good money for the privilege. So they will go to great lengths to support us, often with such quantities of information that we have to search for the nuggets.

How, when and where you are briefed will depend on the complexity of the job, the deadlines involved and your working relationship with the client concerned. In general, copywriting briefs come under the following categories – each, ideally, following the others through in sequence:

- an initial brief
- a client brief

- an agency brief
- a creative brief

The initial brief (outlining the task)

Initial briefs can be as much as a 12-page document or as little as a telephone call. Their purpose is to give you an outline of the task, partly to whet your appetite but also to check that you are:

(a) available, and

(b) willing and able to undertake the job

You may also be asked to quote a fee in advance, based on the amount of time you think the job will take.

Usually, you will be called into the agency or company for a meeting to discuss matters in more detail (as explored in Chapter 5). However, if there is a particularly tight deadline involved, or the task is relatively simple, you may be able to gather all the information you need over the phone and fax (or via emails if you are on the Internet).

The client brief (filling in the details)

This gives you a fuller description of the job and is usually prepared by the company whose product or service you will be promoting. It explains:

- the main objective(s) of the job (i.e. what it needs to achieve)
- the reasons for doing the job (e.g. new research, good/bad publicity, etc)
- whether anything has changed about the product or service
- if any new features or benefits have been added, and why
- what sort of customers are being targeted
- what tone of voice should be used (friendly, informative, serious, etc)
- the type of job required (press advertising, direct mail, PR, etc)
- whether it is to be in colour or black and white
- what size to work to (e.g. full-page advertisement, 6-page leaflet, etc)

- the print run (e.g. how many brochures or leaflets are to be circulated)
- unit costs (e.g. how much each individual brochure or leaflet will cost)
- when the job must be done by

Client briefs are usually supported by background materials such as existing literature about the product or service, details of competitors, any new market research or press articles on the subject, customer testimonials and so forth.

In the absence of a written brief, it can help to type up the notes you take over the phone or during a meeting so that you have a handy reminder to prop up on your desk. If you are writing for an agency, you should also have access to 'contact reports' which confirm details discussed and agreed with the client during meetings.

The agency brief (starting the strategy)

This is prepared by the account director, manager or executive responsible for the client concerned. It is usually intended for internal use, such as briefing other colleagues and creative team members, although some agencies may give a copy to the client if they want to double-check any details or confirm that their thinking is on track.

An agency brief either complements or replaces a client brief and includes extra information such as:

- the account team who will be working on the job
- media or mailing details (where and how the job is to be done)
- any special size or weight restrictions
- client guidelines (e.g. use of their logo, legal disclaimers, etc)
- competitor activity
- deadlines for each stage of the job
- a job or order number (for invoicing)

The creative brief (developing the treatment)

This is a more specific briefing document intended to guide the creative process in the right direction, from copywriting and design through to illustration, photography, Mac work and print. A creative brief may also recommend a particular strategy for tackling the job, such as emphasising one benefit more than another, or focusing on a specific aspect of the offer. It may suggest a humorous treatment, or one that uses high drama to put the message across. Some suggestions could originate from the client, others from the account team or creative director.

If you are given a clear lead about the creative direction to take, it can save a great deal of time in sifting through irrelevant information. However, you still need to be thoroughly familiar with the product and its customers. You might spot a good argument that the agency team has overlooked, or a product feature that was missed out of the client brief.

Woolly briefs

Having dealt with the sensible side of the briefing process, it's worth warning you about an all-too-frequent alternative known in the trade as a 'woolly brief'.

Woolly briefs are those prepared by clients or agencies who either have too many other things on their mind, or simply cannot be bothered with the effort of providing adequate information. At best, they are irritating and time-consuming. At worst, they could reflect a hidden agenda which has a strong impact on how – or even if – you tackle a job.

Typical examples of woolly briefs are gaps in product information or the profile of your target audience. For example, you might be told *when* a product was launched, but not *why*. Did it set a new trend? Was it a radical improvement on others? Has the market changed in some way? Are you targeting a more youthful audience than before? Women rather than men? Factory workers rather than management? And if so, why? These could be important factors in strengthening your arguments.

A working example

Here's how my fictitious aerial challenge at the start of this chapter might look if it was – perish the thought – a real client brief. Spot the 'woollies' . . .

DareDevils Unlimited
Sales Promotion Brief

Objectives: to open up new niche markets for our product by targeting specific professions, starting with those in the creative field.

Product background: DareDevils Unlimited was launched in 1999 as a service to companies, charities and individuals. It combines the excitement of aerial sports with the security of qualified instructors and safety-approved equipment. Services include parachuting, skydiving and bungee jumping.

Special features and benefits: new research has shown that the adrenaline produced during such activities can have a dramatic effect on right-brain thinking and creativity. This offers a valuable opportunity to expand our marketing activities to writers and others of an artistic nature.

Customer profile: male/female writers, all age groups, with particular emphasis on the advertising, marketing and PR professions.

What we require: a full-colour insert for prestigious industry publications such as *Campaign*, *Marketing* and *Marketing Week* with reply-paid coupon and freephone helpline to maximise the response.

First draft copy and visuals: as soon as possible.

What's wrong with it?

- **Woolly objectives:** what do they mean by 'the creative field'? The brief mentions writers, but what about designers, artists, photographers and others? Are they to be targeted separately, or in tandem with writers?
- **Woolly product background:** the client refers to charities as one of the reasons the product was launched but gives no details. This could be a useful selling point in persuading sensible writers to risk their necks. How many charity jumps has the company organised in the past, and with what success?

Can customers name their own charity? Who would be responsible for finding sponsors?

- **Woolly features and benefits:** 'new research' is far too vague to be useful. Who has conducted the research study? Is it independent research, or commissioned by the company? What medical evidence is available to support the findings? The brief also omits the key issue of cost. Is this an expensive sport? Will there be a 'special price' offer? Do people pay a one-off fee or an annual subscription? Should you include a list of prices for individual sports or ask people to contact the client for more details?

- **Woolly customer profile:** given the athletic nature of the sports involved, is it practical to target 'all age groups'? Does the client have clear experience that the sports appeal to such a wide age range? If not, is there an optimum age band that could be targeted more effectively?

- **Woolly job description:** a 'full colour insert' could mean anything. What size should the insert be? How many pages? Should it look like a sales leaflet or an information piece? Will the reply-paid coupon be perforated? Do the target magazines impose any weight restrictions on items like this?

- **Woolly deadline:** how 'soon' is 'possible'? Do they want to see full draft copy or headline concepts only? When is the finished job needed by? Is there a magazine deadline to meet?

If you are working through an agency, they will either raise these questions on your behalf or ask you to phone the client direct. The latter option is usually suggested if your queries are of a complex nature and the account director feels that you are the best person to raise them.

Getting to know your audience

If I had to pick out the single most important aspect of a brief, this would be it. No matter how good a product or service might be, or how much money the client is prepared to pay to promote it, the one thing it has to have is an audience.

Unfortunately, unless you are very lucky, this is often the area where information is at its woolliest. You may be told little more about your readers than:

- their age and income
- whether they are male or female
- what kind of work they do

Even this is usually abbreviated to a list of numbers or letters which lump individuals into 'socio-economic' groups according to their income, working habits or social standing. The two most widely used ranking systems are:

Numbered Rankings (based on jobs, earnings and prospects):

- Class 1 – e.g. company directors, top civil servants, doctors and lawyers
- Class 2 – e.g. junior managers, senior nurses and trade professionals
- Class 3 – e.g. sales managers, computer operators, small businessmen
- Class 4 – e.g. self-employed builders, decorators and driving instructors
- Class 5 – e.g. shop supervisors, plumbers and electricians
- Class 6 – e.g. lorry drivers and assembly line workers
- Class 7 – e.g. labourers, security guards and cleaners
- Class 8 – e.g. those who have never worked and are unlikely to do so

Lettered Rankings (similar but with more emphasis on social class):

- As – upper middle class professionals
- Bs – middle class managerial types
- C1s – e.g. lower middle class clerical workers
- C2s – e.g. skilled working class
- Ds – e.g. unskilled working class
- Es – e.g. casual workers or people on State benefits

Acronyms are also used to describe the buying public. These have now moved beyond the original 'Yuppies' (Young Urban/ Upwardly mobile Professionals), to 'Dinkies' (Double Income, No Kids), 'Woopies' (Well-Off Older People) and various other silly contortions.

Considering these are the people you need to influence, they deserve better. Especially as it is difficult, if not impossible, to write about your subject convincingly without knowing and caring about the individuals it concerns.

Say, for example, you are given the task of persuading young people to start a pension plan. How can you know which buttons to press if all you have is their age, rank and serial number? It might be the most flexible, well managed and high yielding pension in the world, but it will have little impact on a youthful audience unless you know their hopes, dreams and ambitions.

Are they budding entrepreneurs? Do they find it easy or difficult to save? Have they watched their parents or grandparents struggle by on too little money? A few strategic facts on self-employment statistics, savings data and State pension levels could drive all these issues home.

The client or agency you are writing for will be quite prepared to research information like this if you put up a convincing argument of its merit. After all, it is in their interests to give you all the ammunition you need to hit the target they set.

Many copywriters – me included – try to narrow their target audience down to a specific person, then form a picture of that person in their minds. Take this book as a case in point. The opening chapter lists a wide range of people who should find it interesting and informative. But, as I have already mentioned, the book was originally inspired by a small group of writers who were kind enough to show an interest in my work. These are the people who mentally cluster around my desk if I am struggling to explain a particular aspect of the craft.

You could even put yourself in the frame if the subject is one that interests or affects you personally. However, take note of the wealth warning described under 'Avoiding self-seduction'. It's a risk all copywriters run if they are good at their job.

35

Getting the most out of USPs

One of the most persuasive techniques of all is to have something to say about your subject that nobody else can match. Advertisers call it a USP – a unique selling proposition – and your job will be to push such an attribute for all it's worth.

However, 'unique' is a difficult – and potentially dangerous – word to qualify. Few companies can honestly claim to be the only ones to offer a particular product, benefit or service. Occasionally, someone comes up with a new or different way of doing things, but the competition is usually quick to copy – and sometimes improve on – the original. The humble tea bag is a good example, which can now be found in virtually any shape or perforation you care to mention.

So what *does* constitute a USP? Obviously, you will be told about any you can use for a specific job or client – but these are some working examples:

- **Product 'firsts'**: e.g. self-cleaning ovens, non-stick pans, non-drip paint. Anything that makes life less tedious.
- **Safety 'firsts'**: e.g. seat belts, air bags, inflatable passengers. Anything that makes people less vulnerable.
- **Packaging 'firsts'**: milk cartons, bubble wrap, seal wrap. Anything that drives people up the wall trying to open them.

A USP doesn't have to be as dramatic as the above examples. It could be a famous brand name that has become a trade mark for the product it offers: BUPA, IBM, Thomas Cook or Cadbury's for example. Or it could be a special offer, a seasonal novelty or a one-off promotion. It could even be a clever advertising image created for the product, such as a bare-chested hunk downing a diet drink (pause for cold shower).

This last example is a classic case of inventing a USP where none exists. Despite the famous name of the manufacturer, Diet Coke could have become just another diet drink aimed, as most are, at women. The unique proposition in this case is to show a man drinking it and the women admiring the man. Clever.

Maintaining reality

Having set your imagination soaring with USPs, I need to bring you down to earth with a word about governing bodies and codes of practice. The advertising industry is, quite rightly, strictly disciplined. Labelling and packaging are the responsibility of local Trading Standards Departments. Advertising on radio and television is governed by the Radio Authority and Independent Television Commission respectively.

Everything else comes under the aegis of the Advertising Standards Authority. The ASA is responsible for ensuring that the British Codes of Advertising and Sales Promotion are observed and met by everyone who commissions, prepares and publishes:

- newspaper and magazine ads
- posters
- leaflets and circulars
- personally addressed direct mail
- sales promotions
- cinema
- videos
- the Internet
- computer games
- CD-ROMs

The Codes enforced by the ASA require that all these areas of advertising and sales promotion are 'legal, decent, honest and truthful, socially responsible and prepared in line with the principles of fair competition'. This means, fundamentally, that you should avoid:

- insensitive, tasteless or biased materials
- claims with no factual evidence to back them up
- failure to disclose any risks involved

If not, your clients will be made to withdraw the offending item, regardless of how much money has been invested in producing it. This won't enhance your reputation any more than theirs, because even though they bear the ultimate responsibility for advertising and marketing that breaks the rules, they are unlikely to continue using your services if something you write lands them in trouble.

For example, the brief may ask you to make a claim about the popularity of a product, especially in relation to competitive brands. Classic examples include the 'million housewives every day' with Heinz baked beans and '8 out of 10 cat owners prefer it' with Whiskas cat food. These were based on consumer research but not all companies are as scrupulous about backing up their claims. Always check if you are asked to say something impressive without any hard evidence to substantiate it.

The same goes for claims about better performance, higher quality, lower prices or anything else of a comparative nature with other products. If it cannot be proved, it shouldn't be said. And if it can be proved, you must give the source of that proof – e.g. 'Independent market research study carried out by X on behalf of Y.'

Indeed, any statistics you are asked to include should always have a reference source so that people can check the facts independently if they wish. If you are writing about something that could leave the company (or its customers) vulnerable, you may also need to include a warning or disclaimer. For instance, if 'DareDevils Unlimited' was a real company, it would almost certainly have to warn customers in writing about the risks involved to personal safety, and would probably add a disclaimer about its own responsibility in the event of an accident.

One final point about the ASA which is worth noting. Its officers are always happy to offer help and advice if you want to check whether something you are writing complies with the Codes before it goes to print. In fact, they prefer it that way because it saves everyone time, trouble and expense later. It is also reassuring to know that out of an estimated 30 million advertisements and 2.8 billion direct mailings published each year, only 512 were found to break the Codes in the course of a single year (1997). So you have to do something pretty crass to fall foul of the rules.

If you would like to know more about the work of the ASA, including details of recent adjudications, you can visit their website at http://www.asa.org.uk. This is updated monthly and can be downloaded onto your computer for reference.

Alternatively, they can be telephoned on (020) 7580 5555, faxed on (020) 7631 3051, or written to at 2 Torrington Place, London WC1E 7HW.

Guiding and recommending: the writer's role

You need to look at all possible sides of a job to make sure that nothing has been missed which could have an impact on its success.

It might be nothing more than suggesting an alternative way of folding a leaflet for greater impact (see the next chapter), or the addition of customer testimonials to increase the credibility of your offer. As your experience and confidence grows, so will your ability to spot a useful marketing ploy or advertising gimmick.

Recommendations like these can earn you considerable respect with clients and agencies, who will value any suggestions that might add to the creative or strategic approach.

However, you may also need to recommend changes that are of a more sensitive or political nature. This is because copywriters are often closer to – and more informed about – the job than anyone else. Remember all that background information I mentioned earlier? Who else but a writer would take the time and trouble to read it all, or ferret around for extra titbits? And who else would make it their business to talk to as many different people as possible before the job gets underway?

Unless you have worked for a major organisation, you may be surprised how little contact there is between different departments, or how much rivalry can exist. As a result, the approval process for creative work – and especially copy – can take weeks, if not months, while everyone fights their particular corner. This is where writers can play a valuable tactical role, if only by understanding and addressing as many different viewpoints as possible from the outset.

Say, for example, you are briefed by the marketing department of a major brand leader to promote a new product to customers. Marketing people are principally concerned with raising profiles and increasing sales, so the brief will focus strongly on these aspects of the task. The company's legal department will, however, have a very different set of priorities, most of which revolve around keeping the feet of the marketing people on the ground and the customers out of the law courts. Then there's the product development team, who will be furious if the technical brilliance of their wunderkind isn't set out in graphic detail.

How can you keep all these people happy if your brief is to write a small-space ad or a one-page leaflet? You would certainly have a problem fitting everything in without including a magnifying glass as part of the offer. As the writer of the piece, your words will carry weight, so it is easier to guide the client towards a more realistic advertising or marketing vehicle. But don't be fooled into thinking that your first draft will waft effortlessly through the approval process. It won't.

Monitoring the competition

This is not so much fielding off other copywriters – although it is no bad thing to be aware of any rivals for your livelihood – as building a useful reference library of advertising, marketing and press materials. I always try to keep a watchful eye on:

- new advertising campaigns
- fresh slants on an existing campaign
- interesting creative techniques
- press articles
- promotional offers
- companies entering the field for the first time

If you see something that might have a major impact on a client's business, always say so. The odds are that they will already know about it, but they will be impressed to see how well informed you are.

Some companies like to run advertising or marketing campaigns specifically designed to knock the opposition, in which case you will be given access to any competitive offerings. Most tend to prefer the more dignified route of promoting their product or service as the only viable option. Even so, they still need to know how their potential customers are being wooed by others, so anything you can add to their underground intelligence operation will be well received.

Do remember that copywriting is governed by the same rules of plagiarism and copyright as any other kind of writing. You can't merrily lift headlines, body copy, design concepts or anything else from competitive literature and pass them off as your own.

But what you *can* do is read and learn from the persuasive tactics of others and use them to add strength to your own arguments.

Avoiding self-seduction

One of the dangers of being good at your job is that you can easily seduce yourself into buying the very products you are writing about, with disastrous effects on your bank balance. Within a few weeks of working for one agency, I acquired an American Express card, critical illness insurance, private dental cover and an irate bank manager.

The only sure way to remain unmoved about your subject in buying terms is to write about products and services you are never likely to need or want. I have worked on campaigns for operating tables and banana ripening centres – separately of course – without any particular urge to buy either. Unless you plan to specialise in such subjects, the only other deterrent is to pin your latest bank statement to the wall.

Where do you start?

One of the difficulties I have had in planning and writing this book has been deciding which order to present the material. This chapter, for instance, has 'art' in the heading, yet we haven't touched on design, illustration, photography or any of the other creative techniques that are as persuasive as the words they support. But this chapter isn't about creativity. It is about information, the fountain from which creativity flows.

You, too, will have decisions to make about sorting information into the right order. Is this benefit stronger than that? Which facts are more compelling than others? Do you lead with a price advantage or close with it? Clearly, the choices you make will depend on the objectives you have been set in the brief. But there is an even more fundamental starting point: the type of job you have been set and the role it has to play. Press advertising or press release? Leaflet or letter? Invitation or information? Sales or support?

There are so many different types of job that you can – and I hope will – be asked to work on that they deserve a chapter all to themselves.

4. The Tools of Persuasion

In common with many professions, the advertising and marketing world has developed a sub-language which can be baffling to those who are foreign to it. Agencies talk about competing tins of baked beans achieving 'brand differentiation by selective demand advertising' (buy this one, it tastes better), or failing through 'cognitive dissonance' (oh no it doesn't).

There are ways of overcoming language barriers like these, usually by keeping the conversation going long enough to grasp the general meaning. Foreign-sounding copywriting jobs are, however, a tougher area to bluff your way through. It won't look good if you snigger over billing stuffers or bangtails, especially as they are popular methods of including extra sales information in an invoice or statement.

The following is an introduction to commonly used advertising, marketing and promotional methods. I've listed them in alphabetical order for ease of reference, with explanations of any industry jargon that may trip you up during a brief. It isn't an exhaustive list; I haven't, for example, included TV, radio or cinema advertising (too specialised), or printed materials like catalogues (unlikely to need copywriting). Instead, I have concentrated on the jobs that can, and do, turn up regularly in a client or agency brief.

There's always a danger in compiling a list like this, not least because advertising and marketing people delight in creating new names for old tricks. I asked a colleague to check this chapter for accuracy, to which he replied – 'Excellent, but perhaps you should warn your readers that a marketing guru would probably call this a page-based static informer . . .'

All I can say with certainty is that the following jobs turn up regularly in my working life as I hope they will in yours. Words shown in **darker print** (other than headings) indicate a separate entry of their own.

43

Advertorials

A form of **press advertising** which is designed to look like a feature article in a newspaper or magazine.

When used and why: because of their format, advertorials can 'trick' customers into believing they are reading a news story rather than an advertisement. Companies often use advertorials to present a more serious side to their business, sometimes drawing on real or imaginary case studies to illustrate their point. The key advantage in paying for an advertorial rather than sending out a **press release** is that the company can control the style and content of what appears on the page.

Format: 'newsworthy' headlines, supported by a journalistic style of writing. Advertorials must state that they are an 'advertising feature' or 'advertisement' somewhere in the layout, usually above the headline.

Advertising – see under 'Press advertising'

Affinity marketing

Offering a product or service to the customers of one business which is actually supplied and administered by another – 'own brand' travel insurance from a credit card company, for example.

When used and why: many businesses find it more cost-effective to 'buy in' a product or service from a specialist provider than to develop and administer it themselves. By combining skills and resources, they can increase sales, build customer loyalty and add value with the minimum of expense or disruption.

Formats: the process usually starts with a **business-to-business** approach from one company to another, following on with customer promotions once details have been agreed. Big name companies may decide on a joint promotion, although it is more common for the product or service to be offered in the name of the business whose customers are being targeted. This is partly to avoid confusion but mainly to build on existing loyalty factors.

Bangtails – see under 'Envelopes'

Billing stuffers (sometimes called 'statement inserts')

Leaflets which are specifically designed to accompany an invoice or statement and are sent out in the same envelope.

When used and why: billing stuffers can fulfil a number of different functions e.g.

- draw attention to an additional product or service
- highlight a special offer
- impart information about a change to an existing service

Format: the leaflet must fit comfortably into the envelope alongside the main item without adding to the postage costs.

Brand statements – see under 'Straplines'

Brochures and leaflets

The backbone of all businesses, often requiring vast warehouses to store them and expensive mailing operations to distribute them. Can range from a glossy multi-page booklet to a simple folded sheet.

When used and why: brochures and leaflets are used to promote names, reputations, people, products and services. The extent of their power is illustrated by the number of related entries in this chapter.

Formats: there's no particular dividing line between brochures and leaflets, although the latter are usually smaller in size and cheaper to produce. However, there are endless variations in the way they can be designed, both in practical and creative terms:

- **Common sizes:** the A4 letter size (210x297mm) and its half-sister A5 (148x210mm) are widely used for mailing purposes because they fit economically into standard C4 and C5 size envelopes. Equally popular – and for exactly the same reason

– are leaflets measuring one third of A4 (99x210mm) which fit a standard 'DL' **envelope**. The A4 quarter size A6 (105x148mm) is often used for **flyers, inserts** and **outserts**.

- **Bastard sizes:** anything which cannot be cut or folded from a standard A-sized sheet of paper – e.g. a circle or square.
- **'Landscape'** or **'portrait'**: the way the piece will be designed and read, i.e.

Landscape (or sideways)   *Portrait (or upright)*

- **'Stitched'** (i.e. **stapled**) or **'folded'**: how the piece will be finished. Anything more than 8 pages long is usually stapled – often referred to as 'stitching' – while shorter length items tend to be folded (see below).
- **Common folds:** brochures and leaflets can be folded in a multitude of ways to increase their 'interest factor'. However, the examples illustrated on pages 47 and 48 are the most widely used.

Business-to-business promotions

Goods and services promoted by one business to another, rather than to the general public. Methods can range from **trade press advertising** to **letters, direct mail packs, newsletters** and **exhibitions**.

When used and why: some businesses only produce goods that are of interest to other businesses, e.g. manufacturers of large

4-page single fold

6-page roll fold

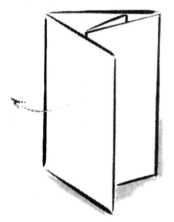

8-page roll fold

6-page gate fold

8-page concertina fold

8-page right-angle (or French) fold

8-page parallel fold

industrial equipment. Others use business-to-business promotions to attract like-minded partners (see **Affinity marketing**) or to support sales outlets (see **Point of sale materials** and **Take-ones**).

Formats: business-to-business promotions use many of the same methods as consumer advertising and marketing. The main differences are in the tone of voice used ('we're both on the same side'), the technical details supplied ('we know what we're talking about') and the financial emphasis ('we can boost your profits').

Competitions

A much-favoured device which can offer anything from a free pen to a new house in the interests of promoting a brand name or product.

When used and why: competitions are a useful means of increasing interest in – and response to – an offer. Other uses include 'awareness raising' promotions (to launch a new company, product or service) and 'list building' exercises (adding new names, addresses and other information to an existing mailing list).

Formats: almost any kind of competition can be used in promotions, although Prize Draws remain a perennial favourite. Others include quizzes – where the answers are usually given within the promotion – and tie-breakers. Competitions that purport to be 'free' must be exactly that, i.e. they cannot be linked with an obligation to buy a product or service first.

Direct mail packs (sometimes called 'direct marketing')

A means of selling goods and services by post to a specially selected audience.

When used and why: companies use direct mail packs for a variety of reasons, but the objective is usually to increase sales of an existing product or draw attention to a new one. The key advantage over TV or **press advertising** is that direct mail narrows an offer down to the people who are most likely to be interested.

Formats: the target audience is chosen from a company's existing customers or from a mailing list supplied by another company or specialist list broker. The selection process is quite sophisticated but, in general terms, it is based on people who have shown an interest in similar products in the past, or who fit a particular profile – e.g. young professionals, early retirers, housewives, sporting enthusiasts, etc. Direct mail packs use many formats, but the most common are:

• an outer **envelope** with a persuasive message to open up the pack

• a one or two-page **letter** addressed to the recipient in person

• a **leaflet** describing the product

• a **flyer** giving details of gifts or other promotional offers

• a means of response, e.g. telephone number or postage-paid envelope

Door drops (sometimes called 'mail drops' or 'leaflet drops')

Printed materials that are distributed through the letterbox, unaddressed, either by normal postal delivery or by hand.

When used and why: door drops are a low-cost way of reaching householders without the expense of buying or developing a mailing list. They are often delivered indiscriminately, although some are targeted to specific postal code areas or house types – advertising materials from local estate agents, for example.

Format: some door drops have outer envelopes which are addressed to 'The Householder' or display an intriguing message, but most are simple devices designed to attract immediate interest. Many include free product samples such as a sachet of shampoo or item of make-up.

Enquiry packs – see under 'Fulfilment packs'

Envelopes

The means by which businesses attract attention to an offer, or make it easier to respond.

When used and why: mailing envelopes – or 'outers' – are a key component of **direct mail packs, mailshots, letters** and other postal sales methods which need to catch the eye quickly. They create the illusion of one-to-one correspondence by addressing recipients in person, often with a compelling message to 'open up and read'. Return envelopes work equally hard inside the pack by providing a pre-addressed, postage-paid method of responding to the offer.

Formats – how 'outers' size up:

- C4 (229x324 mm) for unfolded A4 items
- C5 (162x229 mm) for unfolded A5 items or A4 folded in half
- DL (110x220 mm) for A4 folded into thirds
- C6 (114x162 mm) for A4 folded into four (or A5 folded in half)

Formats– typical return envelopes:

- **BRE** – pre-paid business reply envelope addressed to the sender
- **Freepost** – postage-free reply envelope or address for customers to use
- **Bangtail** – pre-paid reply envelope with tear-off sales piece designed to encourage customers to make an additional purchase or request further information. Often used by book clubs and credit card companies.

Exhibition materials

Promotional items designed to attract stand-holders and visitors to an exhibition or seminar – e.g. trade fairs.

When used and why: exhibitions offer an ideal opportunity for companies to meet their customers face-to-face, or raise staff morale by demonstrating how well their business is doing.

Formats: typical examples include:

- invitation mailings
- pre-event **advertising**
- **press releases**
- exhibitor display materials
- visitor hand-out literature

Flyers

Single or double-sided **leaflets** included with other mailings to highlight a special offer, especially one that has a time limit on it.

When used and why: flyers offer a low cost way of increasing the impact of mailing packs by giving recipients an extra item to read. The longer you can maintain their interest in the pack, the more likely you are to elicit a response. They are also useful for giving information that might change in the near future, such as prices, statistics, special offers and so on. It is much cheaper for a company to change or update a flyer than revise the entire mailing pack.

Formats: flyers are generally designed to work with other items in the pack, so their size or layout may depend on what they are accompanying. However, they also need to stand out and are often designed in a different size or shape from the other materials.

Fulfilment packs (sometimes called 'enquiry packs')

Information sent by post in response to a telephone enquiry or coupon request arising from advertising and other promotions.

When used and why: fulfilment packs are used as a follow-up sales device when a customer's curiosity has been aroused by some other means. Typical examples include information requested via:

- TV and **press advertising**
- **billing stuffers**
- **direct marketing**

- door drops
- inserts and outserts
- take-ones

The main benefits of using fulfilment packs are that they keep the pot boiling in terms of customer interest and continue the sales process. They also (arguably) reduce the risk of expensive materials ending up in the bin because they have been requested rather than sent 'on spec'.

Format: this depends entirely on the nature of the information being sent, but usually features a strongly branded outer envelope (often with a message to say that 'requested materials' are enclosed), a personal letter, a detailed product brochure and an order form. (See also Welcome packs.)

Inserts

Loose leaflets enclosed inside a newspaper or magazine, or additional information enclosed with other mailings.

When used and why: depending on the nature and readership of the publication, inserts offer a comparatively low-cost way of reaching a large number of potential buyers. They are often relatively indiscriminate, with insurance inserts and seed catalogues falling out of the same magazine. However, inserts can also complement the publication in some way (such as double glazing for a mortgage magazine), or ride on the back of a specific editorial feature (such as children's toys for a Christmas issue).

Format: there's no specific design format for inserts, although the publication in which they are to appear may give size and weight guidelines to keep postage costs under control. (See also Billing stuffers, Flyers and Outserts.)

Invitation mailings

These can range from inviting the press to attend a launch party to targeting potential delegates for a seminar or exhibition.

When used and why: invitation mailings are basically a means of ensuring as wide an attendance – and as much publicity – as possible before an event. Shops and leisure clubs often use them to announce private functions designed to increase loyalty among card-holding customers.

Formats: the basic ingredients for an invitation mailing are not much different from any other kind of mailing pack. In general, they include:

- an outer **envelope**, addressed to the recipient in person
- a **letter** explaining the nature, date and time of the function
- an invitation card with RSVP reply slip
- a **leaflet** detailing more about the subject concerned
- a pre-paid RSVP return **envelope**

Leaflets – see under 'Brochures and leaflets'

Letters

The means by which businesses build relationships with their customers, suppliers, sales teams and staff.

When used and why: letters are one of the most persuasive tools of all, because they have a personal touch that few other sales or marketing devices can match. A well-written letter can:

- arouse interest
- build anticipation
- increase loyalty
- demonstrate concern
- overcome resistance
- encourage action

Formats: most letters are either one or two pages in length, although some companies – *Reader's Digest*, for example – will continue a letter over several pages. Some are very simple in layout, while others have colourful design features to lift them out of the ordinary. A heading and postscript are often employed to draw the reader's eye to a key aspect of the letter and encourage a response. Longer letters are usually broken up by sub-heads, centred messages, information boxes and other devices to maintain the reader's interest and attention.

Mailshots

Very similar to **direct mail packs** but can also apply to single **letters, invitation mailings** and other forms of postal advertising.

When used and why: mailshots are invariably used for passing on news of some kind, such as a special offer, fundraising campaign or new product announcement. They are generally a two-step method of contacting customers – i.e. 'complete the enclosed coupon or call this number for further information'.

Formats: usually simple and direct to attract attention quickly. Some form of response device is always included, such as a freephone telephone number or freepost coupon for further information.

Member get member (MGM) mailings

A method of attracting new customers by asking existing ones to introduce friends or family, often with the inducement of a gift or other incentive.

When used and why: MGMs are widely used by clubs, societies and magazines to boost subscriptions, as well as offering a useful marketing tool for businesses in general. Their main appeal is that they are a cost-effective way of reaching a new audience – and because the 'sales pitch' is coming from existing customers, they have a better-than-average chance of success.

Format: usually in three stages –

STAGE 1: promoting the idea to customers, either by writing to them separately or by enclosing a **flyer** with other materials.

STAGE 2: following up any introductions with appealing information about the club, society, magazine, product or whatever.

STAGE 3: acknowledging successful introductions by writing to thank the customer who made the recommendation, together with delivery of any promised gift or incentive.

Newsletters

Journalistic-style communications between a company and its customers, staff, dealer network or anyone else integral to its business.

When used and why: although newsletters purport to convey news, their purpose is more a public relations exercise than anything else. They are a useful means of keeping the company's name at the forefront of a customer's mind, as well as boosting morale among staff and suppliers.

Formats: often quite simple productions on relatively cheap paper, although many are glossy and colourful. The cost of producing and distributing a newsletter obviously has a strong bearing on its format, especially if it is to be a regular feature.

News releases – see under 'Press releases'

Outserts

Promotional offers attached to the front of a magazine, often linked to an article or advertising feature inside.

When used and why: businesses use outserts to draw attention to a special offer, or persuade people to try their products and services on a free trial basis. Because of their prominent front-cover position, outserts can create considerable impact and, unlike **inserts**, are not competing for attention with other promotional items.

Formats: usually dictated by the size and nature of the publication concerned, but can range from **leaflets** to product samples.

Point of sale (POS) materials

Primarily used in shops, these are publicity items designed to draw attention to goods and special offers – for example, 'buy one, get one free'.

When used and why: retail manufacturers face stiff competition within a shop environment, so it's important to make their products stand out as much as possible. Colourful, high impact POS materials such as shelf strips, price cards, dispensers, **posters** and **take-ones** can do much to catch the shopper's eye and a place in the trolley.

Formats: POS materials are strongly branded to the product concerned, using colours and messages that shoppers will recognise. Features usually include prominent prices, special offers and other incentives.

Posters

Promotional devices that range from expensive billboards to staff notice boards.

When used and why: businesses use posters to advertise goods and services, announce events and provide information. They are often used as campaign tools in their own right, especially in public transport areas such as railway stations, subways and bus shelters. Posters are also widely used in banks, building societies, travel agents, surgeries, dentists and benefit offices to draw attention to special features and services. Business promotions, seminars and exhibitions often use posters to build awareness of the event and provide information about times and venues.

Formats: very visual with large headlines, minimal copy and a prominent telephone number or other 'call to action' device.

Press advertising – national, local and trade media

A general description of anything occupying newspaper or magazine space which has been booked and paid for by an advertiser.

When used and why: although press advertising is only one of the weapons in a company's armoury, it is often the first to be wielded. The primary advantage is that it has the potential to reach a very wide target audience. Depending on the objectives of the advertising, companies can:

- increase awareness of their name and product
- attract new customers
- promote new services or product benefits

- impart information
- issue invitations or retractions
- highlight special offers
- announce changes (e.g. mortgage or savings interest rates)

Formats: press advertising usually falls into the following categories:

- *Corporate ads*: focusing more on a company's name, reputation and market strength than the products and services it provides.
- *Coupon ads*: incorporating a money-off voucher or cut-out reply section to encourage immediate response (see also '**Off the page**' ads).
- *Display ads*: advertisements which have a border to distinguish them from others on the same page.
- *Feature ads*: prominent advertisements which dominate the page.
- *Lineage ads*: low-cost advertising that uses words alone without incorporating borders, pictures or other imagery.
- *Off the page ads*: containing enough product information for readers to buy there and then, usually by calling a telephone helpline with credit card details or returning an incorporated order form.
- *Recruitment ads*: attracting new staff by focusing on a company's career prospects, salary, employee benefits, market strengths, etc.
- *Teaser ads*: hinting at something exciting to come without giving too much away (see also **Teaser mailings**).
- *Trade ads*: **business-to-business** advertising in papers or magazines which are specifically written for a particular profession or industry.

Press releases (also called 'News releases')

Newsworthy stories sent to local, national or trade publications for editorial inclusion. Almost anything can be turned into a press release with a little imagination, from product news to human interest stories.

When used and why: press releases are a valuable way for companies to get a 'free plug' in a newspaper or magazine. However, the choice of whether a press release will be used, or how much of it will appear, is down to the news or features editor who receives it. Blatant **advertising** is likely to be binned, but anything with an interesting editorial angle will usually be considered.

Format: the layout of a press release is very important, because it can make the difference between acceptance and rejection by an editor. It should:

- state 'Press Release', 'News Release' or 'Press Information' at the top
- give the date of writing and the date when it can be used (e.g. 'For immediate release' or 'Embargoed until xx/xx/xx')
- lead with a short factual heading conveying the news that follows
- use double spacing between the lines and say 'more follows' at the end of a continuing page
- put 'ends' when the press release copy is finished
- state whether photographs are 'enclosed' or 'following' with size and details – i.e. mono or colour, prints or transparencies – plus a brief explanation of who or what they feature
- conclude with 'Press enquiries to' and give a name and contact number

Reminder mailings

Writing to customers about renewing memberships, or following up invitations and other communications if no response has been received.

When used and why: reminder mailings can prevent the loss of existing customers as well as maintaining pressure on new ones. They are used extensively by companies who rely on regular subscriptions for their business, both as an encouragement to continue and an appeal not to lapse. Reminder mailings are also used in the wake of **direct marketing** campaigns, **invitation mailings** and other written communications if a response is requested but not received.

Format: often just a letter with a pre-paid **envelope** enclosed, although some companies prefer to send the original information for a second time.

Statement inserts – see under 'Billing stuffers'

Straplines (sometimes called 'brand statements')

Short messages accompanying brand names and products which sum up a particular strength or selling point.

When used and why: straplines are an integral part of a company's image and a distinguishing feature of its brand. Worded skilfully, they can leave a lasting impression in customers' minds. Classic examples – past and present – include 'The world's number one airline' (British Airways), 'It's good to talk' (BT), 'That'll do nicely' (American Express) and 'Probably the best lager in the world' (Carlsberg).

Format: short one-liner which often uses a clever play on words and always appears in tandem with the company's name.

Take-ones

Sales **leaflets** designed for public display which encourage people to take one and read it.

When used and why: take-ones are a useful sales tool for High Street-based businesses like banks, building societies, supermarkets and travel agents. They are also widely used by insurance companies and credit card providers in shops, libraries, hospitals and anywhere else the public is likely to visit.

Format: usually a simple 6 or 8-page folded **leaflet** designed to fit within a special holder which stands on a counter or is fixed to a wall. (See also **Point of sale materials**.)

Teaser mailings

Appetite-whetters sent out prior to an **advertising** or **direct marketing** campaign which hint at what's to come without giving too much away.

When used and why: teaser mailings prime an audience by arousing curiosity about the 'main event'. They are often used in the run-up to a new product launch or sales promotion, largely to increase the impact of the campaign when it arrives.

Format: letters and postcards are popular devices, sometimes sent in sequence to keep up the momentum. Other methods include gifts or promotional items linked to the campaign in some way. (See also **Press advertising – teaser ads**.)

Trade press advertising – see under 'Press advertising'

Welcome packs

Information about a newly purchased product, service or membership which enables the customer to benefit from it.

When used and why: welcome packs are widely used by the banking, insurance and credit card industries who need to impart the legal do's and don'ts of their services as well as the benefits. Clubs and societies also send out welcome packs to new members, often repeating the process each time they renew their membership. Major purchases such as cars, computers, kitchen equipment and anything else that needs a set of instructions will usually be accompanied by a welcome pack.

Format: the contents of a welcome pack will depend on the product or service involved, but it might include:

- a covering **letter**
- registration form
- user's guide
- membership card/helpline contact numbers
- guarantee
- information about other products

(See also **Fulfilment packs**.)

5. Tackling the Brief

With a little luck, your first copywriting brief will be a fascinating task which fills you with inspiration and showers you with awards. Then again . . .

However exciting (or otherwise) a copywriting commission might be, it is honestly worth reining in your enthusiasm long enough to think the brief through in a practical and methodical way. You will save time in the long run because you are more likely to get the job right. Even if the deadline is tight, it can be dangerous to rush into the writing process without considering the job from all angles first.

The great thing to remember about copywriting is that it is part of a team event, especially if you are freelancing for an agency. You will be working with talented designers and experienced account handlers who are as keen as you to do a good job. And the thinking process often starts with everyone sitting round the table (or over at the pub) to discuss the brief and the best way of tackling it.

To give you a flavour of what to expect, this chapter is a fly-on-the-wall account of the thinking process behind tackling a brief. We will work from the premise that you are being briefed by an agency and that the 'client' in this case is the company or organisation which has commissioned the agency to do the job. I mention this because the agency itself is your client as they will be paying your bill.

Even if your first brief is a relatively straightforward project, this chapter should still be useful in channelling your thoughts in the right direction. It is divided into three main 'stages':

- **Stage one:** reading the brief
- **Stage two:** a typical agency briefing meeting
- **Stage three:** gathering your thoughts

Stage one: reading the brief

In an ideal world, you would be sent a copy of the brief before being called into the agency to discuss it. If this is the case, give yourself time to read it thoroughly and make notes of any points or questions you would like to raise at the meeting.

Unfortunately, it doesn't always happen this way and your first opportunity to read the brief may be at the meeting itself. If so, don't worry. The odds are that other people will be in the same position, in which case 'time out' will be called to give everyone a chance to read it before the meeting gets underway.

One of the first things you need to know is what kind of job you are being asked to do – i.e. press ad, brochure, leaflet, mailing pack or whatever. Next you want to check how long you have to do it in – i.e. the copy deadline – and the type of 'response' you are being asked to make. You will normally be asked to respond to a brief in one or more of the following ways:

(a) **Initial concepts:** this means you will be developing a range of creative suggestions to help the client decide the best approach for the job. Initial concepts could be invited for a variety of tasks, but they are most commonly requested for projects such as branding exercises (deciding on a name and 'look' for a new product or service), TV commercials and any form of press or postal advertising. The emphasis is on high-impact thinking, i.e. language and imagery designed to appeal instantly to a target audience. A number of options are presented to the client who will either ask for a preferred approach to be developed further, or may decide to put the strongest contenders out to research by showing them to selected consumer groups for their reactions.

(b) **Headlines and copy platforms:** these are often requested for jobs which are more than one page in length – e.g. a brochure or newsletter – or which need further information before they can be written in full. You may still be asked to develop a choice of central concepts, but you will also be providing examples of the other headlines, sub-heads and copy themes that will lead the story forward.

(c) **Full draft copy:** this means, fairly obviously, that you will be writing the briefed task in full. It is a standard request for some jobs – letters, flyers and press releases, for instance – although you may have to write other types of project in one 'hit' if a particularly tight deadline is set.

The ideal brief will give you the opportunity to tackle all three responses in sequence. This gives you and the design team greater scope to develop your creative thinking and experiment with different ideas.

However, as clients invariably leave the briefing process to the last minute, it is more usual to work within deadlines which will either spark an adrenaline rush or an ulcer.

Stage two: a typical agency briefing meeting

These are generally friendly and informal affairs, so there's no need to feel daunted. Nor do you need to dress up for the occasion, other than looking reasonably clean and tidy. The only 'suits' that are likely to attend are the account director or executives, and then only if they are seeing clients that day.

The whole purpose of getting together like this is to help everyone understand the project, so never be shy to ask questions. Colleagues are more likely to be irritated if you don't take full advantage of the meeting than if you do. Remember to take a notepad and pen along with you, or a small tape recorder if you prefer.

It is probably best not to arrive with a laptop, as the constant clicking of keys is likely to drive everyone up the wall.

To give you a greater sense of sitting in on the occasion, I have used conversational-style headings. The lead usually comes from the person chairing the meeting, although anyone is free to join in.

'Is everyone here?'
This tends to be more of a tactical question than an opening courtesy. If a key member of the team is missing – especially someone senior enough to challenge decisions after the event – you could all be wasting your time. It may be more practical to arrange another date when everyone can attend. Otherwise you

could find yourself being asked to develop an alternative approach to the brief later which is neither planned nor budgeted for.
Ideally, the meeting should include:

- a senior member of the client account team – i.e. somebody
  who can answer questions and make decisions
- a project co-ordinator – i.e. somebody responsible for liaising
  with the client and making sure the job runs smoothly
- the creative director – i.e. the agency's top designer or copywriter who will oversee the project from concept stage to
  final production
- a designer or art director – i.e. the person who will be working closest with you in linking words and imagery

'Have we all read the brief?'

Even if a written brief has been sent out in advance of the meeting, agencies are hectic environments where people often have
too much to do and not enough hours in the day to do it. Anyone
who has rushed into the meeting with half an eye on the clock
has probably given the brief little more than a cursory glance,
so it is worth taking a few minutes out while everyone reads it
thoroughly. There's not much hope of a meaningful discussion
if only a handful of people know what they are discussing.

'Do we have a decent product spec?'

If the brief involves a new product, or an update on an existing
one, you will need a detailed breakdown of what it is and how
it works.

This kind of information tends to come in the form of a
product specification – better known as a 'spec' – which tells
you more about the proposition. A typical product spec for an
insurance scheme, for example, would include details such as:

- a table of benefits – i.e. a list of the various 'risks' covered
  and what the scheme will pay or provide in each case
- a subscription table – i.e. a breakdown of what the scheme
  costs to join, depending on details such as age, sex, occupation
  or whatever
- legal information – i.e. disclaimers or facts that have to be
  included by law to protect the company and its customers

- technical information – i.e. an in-depth description of how the scheme works
- competitor information – i.e. details of schemes provided by other companies and how they compare with this one

'What's new?'

The best way to start the creative juices flowing is to have something tasty to bite on, such as an exciting new sales proposition or a fresh slant on an existing one.

This is especially true if the brief has come from a long-standing client, as creativity can wear a little thin over time. Even new clients can pose a familiar challenge because many agencies are chosen on the strength of their experience in certain markets – finance, health or travel, for example. This means you could be writing about the same kind of products again and again, the only difference being the name of the client.

The value of a briefing meeting is that you can thrash out any genuinely 'new' features or benefits to pinpoint the USPs (unique selling propositions). Such as:

- Is this the first of its kind on the market, or merely new to the client?
- Is it an improved version of an existing product or service?
- Is it a departure from the client's usual area of business?
- Is it targeting a new type of audience?

If there is nothing new to say, there may be a different way of putting the same messages across, or a fresh marketing approach that hasn't been used before.

'Is this a branding exercise?'

If the brief involves the launch of a new product or service, the first task might be to create a strong brand image for it.

The principle behind branding products and services is much the same as that for cattle. You have to burn a clear, identifiable mark of ownership onto whatever you are selling to show its pedigree and protect it from being stolen by unscrupulous competitors.

Obviously, it takes the skill of a designer to create the visual 'look' of a top-selling brand. But first you need a brand name –

and that's often the province of a copywriter. There's no set rule for creating brand names because so much depends on the product involved and the copywriter's approach to it. However, a useful starting point could be to write a full description of what the product is or does, then use a process of word elimination to arrive at something punchier. For example, a new dental scheme could graduate from being the 'XYZ Dental Payment Insurance Policy for NHS and private treatment bills' to the 'XYZ Dental Plan' or 'DentAll Cover from XYZ'.

You may also be asked to add a strapline to the name, either to add competitive positioning for the brand or explain what the product does. Our XYZ dental example might, for instance, have the strapline 'Dental health has its benefits' or 'Cash protection for your teeth and gums'.

'Where are we now?'

It's not uncommon for clients to use different agencies to handle various stages of a campaign, in which case you could be cast in a supporting role. Many businesses are prepared to appoint a high profile advertising agency for the media launch but prefer to use an equally trusted – but less expensive – source for follow-up sales and marketing materials.

Continuity is essential in situations like this because you have to prevent the audience from spotting the join. You will need to see preview tapes of forthcoming TV commercials or proof copies of press and poster ads so that you can co-ordinate the creative approach. If they are not available at the meeting, the account manager should be able to give you a verbal synopsis and arrange a viewing as soon as possible afterwards.

Equally, the brief may concern a new phase in an ongoing literature campaign. If so, you will need to tie your thinking process in with any established copy or layout styles. It won't impress the client if you produce a chatty leaflet for a series of crisply worded business guides.

'What are we trying to achieve?'

The ultimate aim of most briefs is to gain more business for the client. But it is the way you go about it that triggers the thought process. For example, if a product or service is flagging, your target might be to:

- strengthen loyalty among existing customers
- attract a different age group
- emphasise a particular aspect of the brand
- focus on people who have specific job or leisure interests
- introduce a new benefit which increases the value for customers

If the brief lists an unrealistic number of objectives, or is vague about what the client wants to achieve, you will have to narrow down the options. Is this a soft sell or hard sell? What sort of buying resistance are you likely to meet? Has there been any good or bad publicity recently? Is price an issue?

These are the sort of discussion points that can turn a woolly brief into a clear strategy. Well, most of the time. If all else fails, you may need to develop alternative propositions as a way of focusing the client's thinking.

'Have we identified the need?'

Most advertising and marketing proposals are based on the premise of 'selling the need'. There's not much point in dwelling on the finer aspects of a product or service if people are not convinced about its relevance to their lives.

'Need' is a fairly loose term in this context: a luxury car, for instance, isn't an essential item in the way that food or shelter is, but could be central to a business entrepreneur who wants to project a successful image to customers or staff.

Although the brief will almost certainly identify a target audience for the proposal, the way you sell the need could be wide open for debate. If we take the same luxury car, the proposition could be:

- the perfect family vehicle because of a greater investment in safety features
- more economical in the long run because it is better engineered and therefore more reliable
- a fitting reward in retirement after years of careful financial planning

'Do we have a free hand?'

Most briefs will have the restraint of a budgetary limit for the time you can spend on it. But you could find your hands tied in other ways, especially if you are working for a client who has a strict set of advertising or marketing guidelines. You might be required to follow a certain formula – e.g.

- headlines or paragraphs of a set length
- a fixed amount of white space (word-free areas) on each page
- preferred words and phrases – 'members' not 'customers' for instance

Details like these will have an impact on how you tackle the job, although you can – and should – still approach it from a fresh and imaginative angle within the guidelines given.

There are other aspects of the brief which could tie your hands in creative terms. You might, for example, be asked to follow the style and format of an existing suite of literature. If so, it is no good coming back with something different because it will simply be rejected. However, if everyone feels that the current literature is not doing justice to the client's business, an alternative approach may be suggested on the proviso that the bulk of the budget is spent on doing what you have been asked.

'Are there any creative no-no's?'

This is the time to find out if similar projects have been tackled in the past which have either not worked or been rejected by the client. Otherwise you could find yourself travelling down a creative route that is doomed to failure from the start.

Equally, if the client is known to have any pet hates – certain words or expressions, for example – you would be well advised to avoid them if you don't want to increase the amount of red ink that comes back on your copy (there will be more than enough without inviting it).

'Any ideas to start us off?'

There is a good chance that someone has already given some thought to the job, even if it is only the person who prepared the brief. So it's worth asking if any ideas have come to mind in the process, either from the account team or the client. These could channel your own thinking into areas that you may not have considered otherwise. If the client has made a contribution to the creative process, you would be well advised to include it as an option if you don't want to offend them.

The simple act of sitting down and talking about the brief will generate useful ideas. Collective thinking is a great stimulant for the imagination and far less inhibiting than staring at a computer screen trying to be creative. At the very least, you and the designer working on the project need to spark ideas off each other. Language and imagery must work together or they don't work at all.

'Can we get away with that?'

Somebody may come up with a really original or unusual idea which is greeted by nervous twitches in certain quarters (usually the account executive who has to sell the concept on to the client).

Off-the-wall creative treatments are great fun, but you need to make sure they are practical, workable and affordable. If they are a departure from the brief, it is usually better to include them as an option than a *fait accompli*.

'Should we develop more than one approach?'

Even if the brief does not include a request for initial concepts, there could be a good argument for putting up more than one idea. If nothing else, it shows how much thought you have put into the proposal.

The creative director usually decides how many approaches should be developed, depending on the nature of the project, the time available and the budget for the job.

By way of an example, you might be asked to think of three alternative front cover headlines for a sales brochure: one focusing on price, one on a key product benefit and one 'teaser' message to intrigue the reader. All three will lead into much the same information inside; it's the 'hook' you hang it on that differs.

'What do we tackle first?'

Bearing in mind what I said at the beginning of this chapter about creativity being a team event, it's essential that everyone has enough time to do their respective jobs within the given deadline. The creative process often starts with the copywriter, so you have to make sure that you don't hold the rest of the team up unnecessarily.

Say, for example, the brief is for a mailing pack comprising a letter, an 8-page leaflet and a 2-sided flyer. All three will require copywriting and design, but not in equal measures. The leaflet and flyer will take longer to design than the letter, so they will need your copywriting input first. You can then work on the letter while the design team is busy with the other two pieces.

A full-scale advertising, marketing and PR campaign is more complicated because you will have media deadlines to meet as well as the design, print and production timetable.

Happily, the logistics are the account team's headache rather than yours – but you *must* stick to the copy dates they give you.

Stage three: gathering your thoughts

You will probably emerge from the meeting buzzing with ideas and keen to start writing. Assuming your next move is homeward, make sure you haven't left anything behind in your enthusiasm. It is always worth running a quick checklist:

• have you got the brief?
• all your notes?
• research materials?
• contact names and phone numbers?
• rough layout sketches?

If you have returned home with quantities of information, you will need to sort it into priority order. I tend to skim through background materials quickly to assess their worth, then read and make notes from any that will have a strong influence on the job.

You may need to contact the client to check your facts or acquire further details about the product concerned. If so, make a list of the questions you want to ask before making the call. It can be embarrassing if you overlook something and have to contact them a second time.

71

Clients tend to get caught up in meetings of their own, so you may not be able to reach the person you need immediately. However, you should have enough information to start work while waiting for them to return your call. If all else fails, get as far as you can and add notes in italics of any details you need to confirm.

Finally – and most importantly – don't let casual callers disturb your train of thought. As most writers know already, one of the drawbacks of working from home is that friends and family can forget it is also your place of business.

Be polite but firm if anyone comes to the door, or calls you up for a chat, and explain that you are working. Alternatively, put the answering machine on – but be ready to grab the receiver if it is a business call.

6. Concepts and Creative Techniques

You probably know the old cliché about agencies running ideas up flagpoles to see if they salute. Heard the one about the Cheshire Cat? If the smile remains, you're on to a winner.

It is certainly true that creative thinking is tried, tested and toasted (or fried) for its strategic strengths. But concepts don't necessarily have to flutter in the wind or wear silly grins to be successful. A factual information leaflet or well-worded brochure are just as much products of conceptual thinking as award-winning press ads. They may not use clever headline techniques or stunning visual treatments – but if they are read and acted upon, the concept has worked.

And that's what it is all about.

This chapter explores a wide range of conceptual techniques, many of which are borrowed from other writing genres. Drama, comedy, tragedy, suspense, even poetry: all feature in a copywriter's thought processes. Each of the techniques described is accompanied by one or more working examples, some taken from real campaigns but most from my imagination. The latter are neither tried nor tested, which means they haven't gone through the normal process of approval by clients, colleagues or professional bodies. Since you will be the sole judge of whether they work or not, I have called them 'test pieces'. Hopefully, this will inspire you to look at them critically and create alternatives for those you reject (or even those you like).

Writing to aunt AIDA

There is a useful formula you can adopt to keep your creative thinking on track. It's called 'AIDA', which stands for:

- Attention
- Interest
- Desire
- Action

Attracting the **attention** of your target audience marks the beginning of your relationship together. And one of the most effective methods is to start at a point of conflict, just as you might in a novel or play. For example:

- A woman's battle against prejudice (*a pension campaign*).
- The plight of a family left behind (*life insurance*).
- An evening ruined and a relationship destroyed (*dandruff shampoo*).

If we take these same three examples, the **interest** and **desire** of the AIDA principle would be:

- The steps women can take to secure a more independent future.
- The relief of a mortgage paid off or school fees continued.
- The confidence of wearing dark clothes without embarrassment.

And the call to **action**?

- Phone now for your *Free Woman* pension pack.
- Take out life cover today and let tomorrow take care of itself.
- Cut out the cost of dandruff with this money-saving coupon.

Although this chapter focuses on aunt AIDA's attention-seeking ploys, it is important to look at the whole picture when working on a concept. If not, you could be left with nowhere to go after your opening gambit.

Take our women's pension campaign as a case in point. You can see that the call to action refers to a 'Free Woman' information pack. If we work backwards from that point, it is easy to see how much mileage can be gained from such a concept. You could lead with the independence factor, or the freedom from financial worries, or the benefit of free information about an important subject. Any of these would be strong contenders for gaining the attention of your audience, but you still have plenty of ammunition to maintain interest and build desire.

Cutting to the chase

Many authors ensnare their readers by starting the action in the middle – or even the end – of the story and then work back to how it all began. The more dramatic or intriguing the opening page, the more likely it is that people will want to read on.

Copywriters also cut to the chase by focusing on the benefit of a product or service and making it relevant to the hopes, fears, desires or ambitions of their target audience. People are more likely to be drawn to something if it captures their imagination and fulfils their needs. Once you have got their attention, then you can hit them with the facts of the matter.

Slimming clubs and diets are a classic case in point. Although many of them do feature 'before and after' pictures, most will lead with a successful 'after' image or something connected with the confidence of losing weight. There's not much mileage in a concept focusing on the misery, hard work and deprivation that leads up to such a point.

This is a fairly obvious example, but the principle can be applied to a variety of conceptual techniques.

Suppose, for example, you are given a brief which seems to offer little in the way of a positive end result, such as a leaflet telling credit card customers that their low introductory interest rate is about to increase. What possible benefit can there be in having to pay more money for something? None of course, but there are ways of softening the blow.

Test Piece

__Client:__ Credit and Loan Bank

__Project:__ Customer mailing – rate increase on 'VisaFlex' card

__Creative treatment:__ Man relaxing in a showroom armchair, a prominent placard nearby with the words: 'SALE ENDS SOON. NOW'S THE TIME FOR VISAFLEX.'

__Headline:__

**Only one of these good things
is coming to an end.**

This is a literal example of starting at the end, but it also illustrates the strength of using a physical benefit or, in this case, a comfort factor to drive your message home. You have turned a negative into a positive by giving your audience a strong reminder of the money they have been able to save with their VisaFlex card, both in terms of purchases and the low introductory interest rate.

You will, of course, have to explain clearly when the rate is increasing and by how much. But the concept also gives you a chance to hero in on all the 'good things' about the card – flexibility, convenience, wide usage, etc – so that your audience will, hopefully, be less inclined to cancel on account of the higher cost.

As most of the examples in this chapter show, words are only part of the conceptual process. Take another look at our VisaFlex test piece: the headline means nothing without the picture to support it. In nearly every case, it is the visual impact of an advertisement or leaflet that catches the eye first – then the message it conveys.

That's why the price of a good copywriter/designer relationship is beyond rubies, malt whisky, chocolate or anything else you value more than life itself.

New slants on old clichés

Best-sellers rely as much today on dashing heroes, courageous heroines and dastardly villains as they always have. What saves them from being clichéd is the discovery of a characteristic you were not expecting, or an outcome to their situation that takes you by surprise.

The whole point about clichés is that when they mean exactly what you expect them to mean, they are boring. Yet there is a certain comfort factor in a cliché, largely because it *is* so familiar. Used cleverly, it draws the eye and lingers in the memory. And the chances are that your audience will remember your message the next time they hear that same cliché used elsewhere. Think of BT's 'It's good to talk'.

We have already used the technique in our credit card test piece by adapting 'all good things must come to an end'. Here's another:

Test Piece

Client: Quality Wallcoverings

Project: Press ad for the 'Welcome Wallpaper' range

Creative treatment: A half-decorated room with a rip in one of the newly papered walls and a shattered photograph lying on the floor below.

Headline:

**You patch up the quarrel.
We'll paper over the cracks.**

You have taken a relatively dull product and placed it at the heart of a drama. The phrase 'papering over the cracks' is a cliché – and a negative one at that – but there is a positive twist to save it. The reader can see the torn wallpaper, so it's clear that this is the crack which will be papered over. Even the well-worn phrase 'patched up' works hard with the damaged wallpaper and photograph.

Naturally, you will include a further illustration to show the room fully decorated, a repaired photograph on the wall and perhaps a freshly delivered bouquet of flowers to show that harmony has been restored.

More Test Pieces

'A close shave'

Use this as a straightforward description of something razor sharp or risky and it's a cliché. But give it a visual twist and you have a concept. How about a leaflet for a woodworking tool which shows Count Dracula confronted by a smooth and deadly wooden stake?

Smith's Power Tools. Dead sharp for a close shave.

'When push comes to shove'

Put this in a headline in its accepted sense – e.g. 'When push comes to shove, you'll be glad you chose brand X' – and you have a hopeless cliché. But if you use it in a literal sense to promote, say, a shelter for abused women, it becomes a powerful and emotive message.

CrisisPoint. When push comes to shove, we're here to help.

'Getting along famously'

I used this as a working example when running a copywriting course at the much-loved and highly regarded Writers' Summer School, Swanwick. For six magical days every August, hundreds of writers ranging from household names to raw beginners support, encourage and learn from each other. This book is a direct result of the confidence it inspires to try something new. So it was a logical move to suggest this variation on a theme:

Come along to Swanwick, where writers get on famously.

Pun intended

Comedy writers often make clever use of puns, especially in the titles of their books and plays. They have the skill and professionalism to do so. But puns are, in my view, best avoided by copywriters because we cannot soften them over the course of several chapters or acts. The only effect we achieve is to make our audience cringe, especially if an exclamation mark is added to drive the 'joke' home.

But I want to address as many creative techniques as possible in this chapter – and some copywriters do use a change of word or spelling to put a twist on a familiar phrase, often with considerable success. Here are some I have made up with the help of my *Dictionary of Clichés* and *Penguin Dictionary of English Idioms*.

Test Pieces

**Felix 'n' Fido Sovereign Blend.
A royal feast for reigning cats and dogs.**

It's Pa for the Course this Father's Day.
Give Dad a golfing gift voucher.

You'll get value in spades
at GreenLawns Garden Centre.

I will leave you to be the judge of whether these work or not.

Colourful characters

Creating fictional characters is a technique regularly borrowed
from literature by copywriters to humanise an advertising or
marketing campaign. Remember Beattie and her 'ologies' from
the BT television ads? Or the Oxo family? But characters don't
have to be fictitious – or even human – to qualify as colourful.
Think of the Dulux dog and Andrex puppies.

Television is a natural medium for conceptual techniques like
these. Yet colourful characters can also be used successfully in
brochures, mailers and other written communications to act out
our messages for us.

Test Piece

Client: A & B Ergonomic Offices

Project: Business-to-business brochure for the Desirable
Desking range

Creative treatment: Brochure front cover showing woman
sitting at executive desk, feet up, wine glass in hand, talking on the telephone.

Headline:
This is Sally Anderson.
She's far too busy to leave her desk.

The concept introduces an obviously successful businesswoman
but with an intriguing premise. She doesn't appear to be particularly busy – so why can't she leave her desk? The brochure will
reveal that this is no ordinary desk but one from the Desirable
Desking range. Who could possibly bear to tear themselves
away from such a beautiful item?

You could extend this concept to a full-scale 'Sally' campaign, from showroom posters and price cards to door drops and direct mail packs.

The attraction of opposites

Pitching apparently ill-matched characters against each other and then developing a relationship between them is a popular technique in short stories and romantic fiction. It can be an equally effective copywriting tool when applied to language and imagery.

Take our 'Sally Anderson' test piece. The picture said one thing, the words another. By creating an intriguing disparity between the two, the interest factor increases and the audience is persuaded to see what happens next. Here's another example of pitching headline and visual against each other.

Test Piece

<u>Client:</u> BetterBuild Homes

<u>Project:</u> Showhome flyer promoting price reductions on selected plots

<u>Creative treatment:</u> brand new house in course of construction.

<u>Headline:</u>

This house is coming down.

Why would a house that's clearly going up be described as coming down? The answer will lie in a prominent reference to the reduced cost of buying this exciting new home. There is no need to include pictures of a completed house in the visual because the flyer is going on display in the Showhome and visitors will be surrounded by evidence of what the finished homes look like. If it was a press ad or other type of 'remote' promotion, you would have to feature a fully constructed house as well as the part-finished one so that your audience can see what a desirable residence it will eventually become.

Antonyms are another effective way of using opposites to attract. One of the best examples I've seen of this particular tech-

nique was on a crime prevention poster in a high street shop window with the message: 'Heard a whisper? Give us a shout.'
Here are some of my own:

Test Pieces

A big moment on the small screen.
(famous film clip illustrated on a wide-screen TV system)

Hot stuff for colds.
(honey and lemon flu remedy)

The long and short of healthy eating.
(pasta)

We're near when you're far.
(travel insurance)

Twists and turns

Mystery and crime writers delight in surprising their readers with unusual twists and unexpected turns. The idea is to keep them hooked until the final word has been read. Copywriters apply similar techniques with much the same motive.

One of the most widely-used is word association. Take a look through your post or a newspaper and see how many leaflets and headlines use a clever play on words to add interest or intrigue. The trick is to use a word that combines different grammatical functions – a noun which is also a verb, for example – so that it has a double meaning.

Test Pieces

See your dentist regularly. It's a really good practice.

Get fresh with your greengrocer.

Open to the need for extra home security?

There's no holding our self-defence classes.

Each of these would develop nicely into an ad, leaflet or poster for the service described, most of which are of the 'friendly local supplier' variety. But you can also use a more sophisticated form of word association if the job requires. I created the concept 'Accounting for Health' for a client who wanted to drive home the message that staff sickness costs money. Another asked me to think of a positive way of alerting women to the impact of the State pension age changing from 60 to 65 and what they could do to protect their future. 'A new age for women' was born.

It isn't only word-play that can create twists and turns in headlines. You can use whole sentences that appear to be saying one thing but actually mean another. Here's an example:

Test Piece

Client: SureSafe Surgical Equipment

Project: Direct mail pack for Multi-Pro operating table

Creative treatment: Flat-line on heart monitor, patient just in view on operating table.

First headline (front cover):
It was lucky he died today.

Second headline (inside):
His surgeon had the technology of a Multi-Pro table to save him.

This is a good example of using a split message to heighten impact. We will be looking at this technique some more, but in the meantime you might be wondering how an operating table can bring someone back to life and how I know about such things.

The truth is that although I have invented this concept as a chapter illustration, I have also written in the past for a surgical equipment supply company. One of the first things the client insisted upon was that I not only had a working demonstration of an operating table – with a model, I should add, not a patient – but that I also understood the importance of why it had the features it did. Among them was a button which instantly swung the table to a different angle if the patient suffered breathing difficulties during an operation.

All of which our fictional direct mail pack would address, although in somewhat more technical terms (surgeons wouldn't appreciate a lesson in Trendelenburg manoeuvres).

Keep people in suspense . . .

How do playwrights entice an audience out of the bar after the interval? Or novelists persuade you to read another chapter, even though it is three in the morning? By introducing a cliffhanger.

In advertising and marketing, it's known as a 'teaser'. There are numerous ways of applying the technique, one of which is to use a split headline (as shown in our operating table test piece). This really only works if the two headlines are on different pages; there's not much suspense if the audience can see the pay-off without having to do anything to sate their curiosity.

Split headlines can be done as two separate sentences, as in our test piece, or as a single sentence which continues from one page to another. The latter is usually indicated by the use of three dots (it should never be more or fewer than three) which either come at the end of the first split or the beginning of the second. For instance:

Test Piece

Client: Go Further Travel Agents

Project: Full colour teaser ad for Concorde weekend break

Creative treatment (first hit): Cloudless sky with Concorde nose tip edging into the side of the picture.

Headline:
Some of the best ideas

Creative treatment (second hit): Concorde in full view over the Manhattan skyline.

Pay-off headline (follow-on page):
. . . come out of the clear blue sky.
(We have a nose for these things.)

This example relies as much on the split visual as it does on the continuing headline. It might work in a leaflet, but it would be better as a press ad run over two consecutive pages. Teaser mailings use a different technique. The tease is in the lack of information rather than the lack of a completed sentence.

If we use our same Concorde holiday scenario, a typical teaser mailing could take the form of a 'wish you were here?' postcard from America. The front of the postcard might feature our clear blue sky and Concorde nose tip, or even the Manhattan skyline with the nose tip in view. The back would simply have the recipient's name and address and a brief appetite-whetter about shopping or sight-seeing in New York, printed in such a way that it looks hand-written – just as a postcard would be.

After a few days, a second postcard might arrive to increase the suspense, followed finally by a leaflet from the holiday company explaining what it is all about.

Rhyme and rhythm

It isn't only poets and song-writers who apply a musical resonance to their use of language. Copywriters regularly inject rhyme and rhythm into their words to make them more memorable (alliteration is another favourite method).

Advertising jingles are an obvious – and often irritating – example of combining both techniques. But there are ways of using one or the other to soften a message or increase impact. I saw a good example of a rhyming headline in my GP's waiting-room recently on a poster designed to dissuade patients from calling the doctor out at night. The message was 'Be nice, think twice'. Others that you may have seen over the years include 'Use it, don't lose it' (your vote) and 'Watch out, there's a thief about' (police information).

I mentioned alliteration earlier. It is a useful – and much-used – headline device, although care needs to be taken not to overdo it. Given the link with poetic techniques, perhaps it isn't surprising that alliterative headlines tend to have a distinct beat to the bar.

Test Piece

<u>Client:</u> Slim 'n' Healthy Fitness Clubs

<u>Project:</u> Advertorial for new five-step slimming plan

<u>Headline:</u>
Sensible slimming in five easy steps.

Note that I haven't suggested a creative treatment for this concept. This is because the project is an advertorial and the whole idea of these is to make them look as much like an editorial article – and as little like an advert – as possible.

Do you see what I mean about a rhythmic beat? It is quite difficult to say this headline out loud without chanting it. I could have extended the alliterative 's' by saying 'simple' rather than 'easy' but it would have over-egged the pudding (and spoilt the rhythm).

More Test Pieces

Fresh fish. The family favourite.

Luscious tights for lucky legs.

Wood works wonders for winter.

Point of view

Every author has to decide the principal character from whose point of view the story will be told. Copywriters adopt a similar discipline, except that our 'principal characters' are often inanimate (i.e. when the product or service is the hero of the piece). However, there is a popular character in the copywriter's pack who frequently makes his or her presence felt: the person reading the message.

It's known as the 'you' factor. By talking directly to your audience, you can make your words powerful, personal and relevant. Here are some examples of headlines with and without the 'you' factor.

Test Pieces

[Without]	We couldn't have done it without our customers.
[With]	We couldn't have done it without *you*.
[Without]	Our tissues are tough on colds.
[With]	Our tissues are tough on *your* cold.
[Without]	Everybody loves a FlyAway holiday.
[With]	*You'll* love a FlyAway holiday.
[Without]	Smoke detectors can save lives.
[With]	Smoke detectors can save *your* life.

Point made?

Don't lose sight of the plot

It isn't only novelists who run the risk of becoming so enmeshed with clever twists or extra characters that the story runs away from them. Copywriters are equally capable of losing sight of the plot or, in our case, the brief.

If you have something important to say, say it. More often than not, that is the best and most successful technique of all. Above all, make sure that the conceptual approach you take is appropriate for the task in hand. If you are writing an inform-ation piece, an equally informative heading is more suitable than something which makes a clever play on words or leaves the reader guessing. If the subject is of a sensitive nature – funeral planning or health screening, for example – you want your words to be warm and understanding, not crisp and smart.

There are three important points to remember about con-cepts and creative techniques: (1) the brief, (2) the brief and (3) the brief. If you have answered all three, you have cracked the job.

A disclaimer to finish

Advertising and marketing materials frequently bristle with final phrases aimed at getting the client out of trouble if anyone challenges the information.

So, in the best traditions of wriggling at the end, I would like to point out that the 'test pieces' contained in this chapter – and the client names accompanying them – are, to the best of my knowledge and belief, straight out of my little grey cells. But it is always possible that some unscrupulous person thought of them first. If so, I apologise unreservedly for having a similarly fertile imagination.

7. Style, Structure and Revision

In the course of planning this book, it seemed natural to include a chapter on style. Isn't that what every writer strives to achieve?

But how can you define style? Or teach it? Copywriters are as individual as any other kind of writer in the way we work and think. Give the same brief to three of us and we'll come back with three different ways of putting the message across. If each version answers the brief with freshness and originality, which one has – or hasn't – got style?

Determined to be helpful, I turned to other writers for inspiration. Voltaire: 'All styles are good except the tiresome sort.' I'll go along with that. Wilde: 'In matters of grave importance, style, not sincerity, is the vital thing.' Hmm. Swift: 'Proper words in proper places make the true definition of style.' Very possibly, but not in advertising and marketing which regularly breaks most of the rules in the interests of – well – style.

With relief, I discovered that my friend and fellow A & C Black author, Jill Dick, shares my perplexity about defining style. Her chapter on the subject in the second edition of *Freelance Writing for Newspapers* starts: '"He writes with such style," glowed a popular columnist's admirer. All I really understand from such a remark is that the speaker enjoys reading work written with what he calls style. What style *is* – in that sense – I don't know. I do know that thought must be structured before writing can be, and that there is a deal of nonsense written and spoken about style.'

Absolutely.

It seems to me that style is inseparable from structure – and revision is essential for both. So the most practical way to deal with all three is to move from the abstract to the actual by exploring various styles you can introduce into – and extract from – your copy to keep it fresh, crisp and interesting.

We will use 'test piece' examples, as in the last chapter, to show the different techniques in action. But first a word about stylistic dingbats and routine rule-benders.

Cardinal sins and acceptable lapses

I mentioned earlier in reference to Swift's quote that many of the rules about proper words in proper places are broken on a regular basis in advertising and marketing. But there are – thankfully – some aspects of English language usage that remain sacrosanct, even for copywriters.

Misspelt, mis-apostrophe'd or misplaced words are cardinal sins, the penance for which is an immediate lack of work. Like this, for instance:

The copy draught went down a storm and the client got in the drink. Being a gin and tonic, I decided to celebrate. Thats when the cat got it's pause on my prose.

I won't insult you by pointing out the errors. The real object of the exercise is to show that you can't always rely on dictionaries or computer spell-checkers to get you out of trouble. They have a sneaky habit of hiding in a corner, grinning, while you make an idiot of yourself. By way of evidence, I ran my Apple Mac spell-check program over the above and the only query it raised was 'thats' (no apostrophe between the 't' and the 's').

All of which proves that a working knowledge of the rules is essential before you can think about bending them. If you want further evidence, look through your post and see how many letters soliciting your custom start with the phrase: 'As a valued customer, I wanted you to know . . .' So who's the valued customer then?

Now for the rules you *can* bend. Copywriters have scant regard for purist views on prepositions. Finishing sentences with 'in', 'on', 'about', 'up' or 'with' may not be grammatically correct but it keeps them short, simple and to the point. (A lesson illustrated by Churchill's much-quoted example of 'the sort of English up with which I will not put.')

As for conjunctions, we regularly start sentences with 'because', 'and', 'but' and 'which'. Because even though it breaks all the rules, it keeps our copy crisp. And that's what we are paid to do. But remember the importance of structuring your copy. Which brings us to the next part of this chapter – and an end to the lesson on sentences beginning 'because', 'and', 'but' and 'which'.

Where does it all start and end?

Remember the point I made about giving the same brief to three copywriters and the different ways they are likely to respond? If they're worth their salt, there will also be some important comparisons. Each will, or should, answer the brief in detail. And each will use a strong opening gambit, a persuasive central argument and a compelling finish.

Or, put another way, their work will have a beginning, middle and end.

This simple rule is as relevant to structuring copy as it is to any other kind of writing. No matter how skilfully you hook the attention of your audience at the start, the real test is sustaining their interest long enough to achieve the desired result. By structuring the way you approach each job, you are less likely to start with a bang and finish with a whimper.

You might find it helpful to revisit someone we met in the last chapter. Remember aunt AIDA?

- <u>A</u>ttention
- <u>I</u>nterest
- <u>D</u>esire
- <u>A</u>ction

Although acronyms are useful as memory-joggers, they can sometimes be misleading. Think of all those enticing 'buy one, get one free' offers in your local supermarket which rejoice in the shortened form of BOGOF. Aunt AIDA might project a cosy image of cough drops and camomile tea, but she's closer to Checkpoint Charlie in character: challenge the system and expect rapid gunfire. I haven't worked out a suitable acronym for this, but one of the 'Cs' could surely stand for copywriting (suggestions on a wine label, please).

The point is that you need a strategy if you are to persuade people that your words are credible. If not, they will shoot you down without mercy. Every word you write must be relevant to the person reading it so that they identify with what you are saying.

Here's an example of AIDA in action, taken from a copywriting course I ran at the Writers' Summer School, Swanwick. As I mentioned in the previous chapter, the School attracts people from a wide range of backgrounds and interests. Some have already achieved success in their writing careers, but many more are just setting out. All share the frustrations that writing for a living can produce and enjoy exploring new avenues for their talents. But the greatest attraction of Swanwick is the opportunity to be in the company of like-minded friends in a peaceful and beautiful Derbyshire setting.

The test piece you are about to see was based on all these identifiable audience benefits.

Test Piece

<u>Project:</u> 'Awareness' advertising

<u>Headline:</u>

Is your writing going nowhere?
[Attention]

<u>Body copy:</u>

Writing can be a lonely business. Ask any novelist, poet or playwright. *[Interest]*

In fact, why not ask biographers, journalists, copywriters, comedy writers, crime writers and short story writers? You'll find them all relaxing at the Writers' Summer School, Swanwick, this August. *[Desire]*

Give yourself a break. Come along to Swanwick, where writers get on famously.

Call us now on *[telephone]* or email us at *[mailbox]*.
[Action]

Analysis
The headline is deliberately targeted at would-be writers because they are likely to be the most fruitful audience in terms of

attracting new members. Most full-time writers would know about Swanwick already, either by word of mouth or through publications like *The Author* and *Writers' News*.

Note the contraction of 'you will' to 'you'll'. Copy tends to adopt spoken rather than written English. It's something I've had to unlearn during the writing of this book (not always successfully, as you can see from this sentence).

Extending the principle

Suppose we take the same Swanwick proposition and apply it to different forms of advertising. A leaflet insert, say, in a Sunday supplement.

We could modify the headline concept to act as a 'teaser' designed to encourage people to pick up – and open – the leaflet. But the supporting structure now needs to fill pages rather than paragraphs. And the extended copy must continue to maintain your audience's interest, build their desire and prompt them to take action.

What else can we say about our subject? Now that we have the luxury of more space, we can afford to pay the headline off in greater detail – e.g.

- The attraction of a holiday in good company and beautiful surroundings.
- The educational benefits of meeting and talking with other writers.
- The inspiration of attending talks, courses and lectures by established professionals in many writing genres.

Naturally, the design of the leaflet will also play a major role in attracting attention to our proposition by building visual images to support the messages.

Test Piece

<u>Project:</u> 4-page A5 'awareness' insert

<u>Front cover headline:</u>

If your writing's going nowhere . . .

Inside spread (continuing headline):
give yourself a break at the
Writers' Summer School, Swanwick.

Body copy:

Writing can be a tiring business at times, not to mention a lonely one. Who else labours alone for days over carefully crafted work, only to have it fall into unappreciative hands?

Other writers, that's who. And you'll find them relaxing and enjoying each other's company at the Writers' Summer School this August. Short story writers, novelists, journalists, copywriters, playwrights, poets, biographers . . . all with stories to tell and experiences to share.

A wonderful learning environment

The Writers' Summer School lies in acres of private parkland in the Derbyshire village of Swanwick. Sweeping lawns surround the main house and conference rooms, while a swimming pool, bar, shop, book room and chapel are among the many facilities designed for quiet enjoyment and relaxation.

But this is a place that also buzzes with excitement and activity all through the day. Here you can benefit from:

- fascinating talks by famous writers
- practical courses in all the genres
- workshops and discussion groups
- one-to-one surgeries with successful writers

Want to know more?

The Writers' Summer School will be running from xx to xx August this year. Double and single rooms are available, many with en-suite bathrooms. Prices range from £xxx to £xxx.

For full details and a priority booking form, just give us a call *[telephone number]* or email us on *[mailbox]*.

Come along to Swanwick, where writers get on
famously.

Analysis

Does our leaflet pass the AIDA test? Remember we only have a matter of seconds to catch the attention of our audience.

The opening teaser headline should be intriguing enough to persuade people to open the leaflet, and there's a good conceptual play on words with the use of 'give yourself a break' on the continuing headline inside.

So far, so good. Our next task is to maintain the interest we have aroused: does the opening paragraph achieve this? It starts on a relatively negative note – loneliness and frustration – but these are emotions that will strike a chord with many writers, especially those who have yet to make their mark. The copy switches immediately to a more upbeat tone. Friendship, relaxation, fascinating company, shared experiences. The desire is beginning to build.

We keep up the momentum with mouth-watering descriptions of the conference setting and facilities, then increase the pace with words like 'buzzes', 'excitement' and 'activity'.

Now for the climax of the piece: all the wonderful opportunities for our audience to learn from experienced and successful writers. Who could resist booking a place immediately? We need to make it easy for people to respond, so the prominence of the call to action is increased by putting the phone number and email address on a separate line in large, bold print.

Finally, we bring the concept back full circle by paying off the 'going nowhere' front cover with a triumphant strapline linking Swanwick with friendship and fame.

Hopefully, they're hooked.

Getting the tone of voice right

Although we touched on this subject in earlier chapters, it is such a vital aspect of the job that I want to address it in more detail before going any further with this one.

The way you talk to your target audience is the influencing factor in whether they take you seriously or not. If the tone of voice is wrong, the entire message can be lost. A simple way to judge whether your copy hits the right tone is to put it in the context of a spoken conversation. If you are passing on good news to a friend, you would do so in a chatty way rather than giving them a businesslike report. If the news is of a more serious nature, the chattiness would give way to sincerity and concern. And if you are discussing something important with a business colleague or somebody in authority, your manner would reflect the efficiency and professionalism they expect of you.

So it is in copy. The tone of voice you adopt in your writing has to be appropriate to the subject and the person reading it.

Our Swanwick test pieces are of the 'good news to a friend' variety. The tone is warm and informal: a me-to-you message of enthusiasm and encouragement. But what if we change the target audience and the objective of the job? Say, for example, the leaflet is part of an invitation mailing to professional speakers inviting them to give a talk at the conference. Their time is valuable and their success places them much in demand as speakers.

The tone of voice and style of the copy must change accordingly. It needs to become more factual and businesslike to persuade our target audience that this is a worthwhile venue for a guest appearance.

NB: The following test piece is purely for illustration. Arrangements between guest speakers and the School are entirely private, so the only aspect of the 'proposition' that I know for a fact is the celebrated reputation and longevity of the School.

Test Piece

<u>Project:</u> 4-page A5 invitation mailing leaflet

<u>Front cover headline:</u>

**The Writers' Summer School, Swanwick –
a fitting platform for success stories.**

<u>Inside spread (main headline):</u>

Can you pass on the benefit of your experience?

<u>Body copy:</u>

Every year, hundreds of writers and would-be writers head for Swanwick to share stories, experiences and comradeship.

But the main event is, unquestionably, the opportunity to hear celebrated guest speakers talk about their work and the path that led to their success.

Speakers such as yourself.

A renowned and respected venue
Swanwick is not only the longest established writers' conference in the country but also the best known. And, indisputably, the best loved. Members return year after year, refreshed and renewed by their experiences.

Comfort and privacy during your stay
Guest speakers are accommodated overnight in complimentary suites with private bathroom, telephone and TV. Evening meal and breakfast, also at our expense, is served at the Chairman's table, where speakers are joined by Committee members and other well-known writers attending the school.

Past speakers at Swanwick include:

- Ruth Rendall
- Bernard Cornwell
- Kit Wright
- Norman Wisdom

Please say yes . . .
Your presence at this year's conference would be both a privilege and pleasure. Won't you please say yes?

An appropriate fee is, of course, payable for your time.

For details of days, times and dates to match with your diary, please call or email the Secretary on [telephone number] / [mailbox].

Analysis
Quite a change of approach, isn't it? Gone is the emphasis on holiday atmosphere and cheery companionship; in its place, a serious business proposition pitched at a professional audience.

The language, structure and content of the piece reflect this altered perspective. But the AIDA principle still applies.

Attention is captured by the twinning of 'fitting platform' and 'success stories' on the front cover, supported no doubt with a well-known past speaker pictured on stage before an entranced audience.

Inside, the headline is respectful with a hint of challenge (note the use of 'can you' rather than 'will you'). Interest is maintained by the body copy leading immediately into the numbers of people attending and the 'unquestionably' strong focus on the importance of guest speakers.

Desire starts to build with the positioning of the conference as 'longest established', 'best known', 'indisputably best loved', all of which underline the 'fitting platform' concept on the front cover.

Now we come to the real persuaders: that impressive list of past speakers, the promise of luxurious free accommodation, a place of honour at the Chairman's table and, of course, the promised fee. The call to action drops the informality of 'us' in favour of 'the Secretary', but still uses a separate line to make the phone number and mailbox details prominently visible.

Interesting devices

Sales copy has to work really hard to hold the reader's interest. The lengthier the piece, the tougher it gets. Product brochures, for example, frequently run to 16 pages or more in length. How do you sustain interest with a challenge like that?

There are a number of devices you can introduce to break your copy up into readable chunks. Bullet-pointed lists inserted between paragraphs are an obvious ploy because:

- they enable people to get at the facts quickly
- they can be printed in coloured panels for added impact
- they can be used to draw attention to USPs

Much the same effect can be achieved with 'Did you know?' panels.

> **Did you know** . . . that breaking copy up like this is an excellent way of holding your audience's interest?

If the budget allows, you can 'hide' copy by adding an extra folded panel to the page which has to be opened out to read. Or by including a peel-off card with a telephone number for handy reference and a hidden message beneath.

Here are some more tricks of the trade.

Bring in a case study

This is the copywriter's equivalent of the 'show don't tell' philosophy, except that you do both.

Say, for example, you are writing a brochure about a private medical scheme. The client has asked you to focus strongly on the benefits of avoiding lengthy NHS waiting lists and receiving treatment promptly in privacy and comfort.

All these facts can – and should – be put across convincingly in headlines and body copy, but if you show an example of somebody actually benefiting from them, the impact increases immediately. Unless space is tight, it is usual to show at least two case studies so that contrasting personal situations can be illustrated.

Test Pieces

<u>Project:</u> Two illustrative case studies for the FastCare Private Medical Scheme

<u>First case study (work-related):</u>

We didn't add a wait to John's worries.

<u>Body copy:</u>

John Chandler couldn't afford the risk of waiting months for an operation on his back because his copywriting business would suffer just as much as he would. He rang our medical helpline and we arranged for him to go into hospital the following week. His private room had a bedside telephone, so he kept in touch with clients while regaining his health and strength.

Second case study (family-oriented):
Sophie needed to hear that she wasn't alone.

Body copy:
3-year old Sophie's parents, Peter and Anne, were horrified when their GP told them she needed an operation on her ears. She seemed so little to be in a hospital bed. We recommended a local private hospital that specialises in children's illnesses. Anne stayed with Sophie all the time she was in hospital and Peter rearranged his work schedule so that he could visit as often as possible.

Analysis
The headline in the first case study is technically a pun, but an acceptable one. The word 'wait' is appropriate in the context of what follows, even though there is an obvious link with a 'weight of worry'. The second case study also uses a play on words, but in a gentler way to make it more appropriate to the subject.

The tone of voice used in each case study changes to reflect the difference in vulnerability of our two patients. First we have John, a man with a bad back and a business to run. The copy is equally businesslike, explaining the steps he took to solve the problem. Then we have Sophie and the more emotive theme of a child's illness. The language becomes more personal: the parents are 'horrified', the patient 'so little'. Both case studies answer the client's brief to the letter, but in very different styles.

Introduce a crisis

Human emotion is a powerful sales tool. When you introduce fear, tension or anxiety into your readers' minds, they'll not only identify with your words – but also keep reading to see how your story ends.

The danger in using a strong or dramatic theme is that you could veer into purple prose. Resist with all your might. Simple, understated language has far more impact. Let your headlines shock or worry your readers, but don't leave them so breathless with your copy that they need a strong drink to recover. If they do, you've lost them.

Test Piece

Project: Credit card statement insert for GentleRise Stairlifts

Headline:

"Help. I'm trapped in my own home . . ."

Body copy:

Has your home become a prison because you can no longer manage the stairs? Moving house is one solution, but could you bear the upheaval? Especially if it means leaving treasured memories behind.

Regain your freedom with a GentleRise stairlift
Now your home can be your own again. A GentleRise stairlift can be fitted to virtually any staircase with the minimum of fuss. And it has an impressive range of safety features for added confidence.

One free phone call is all it takes
There's no pressure or hard-sell with GentleRise Stairlifts. Call our friendly helpline now – we'll pay for the call.

[Freephone telephone number]

Analysis
See how the copy style moves from emotive words like 'trapped', 'prison', 'bear' and 'treasured' to the reassurance of 'minimum of fuss', 'impressive range of safety features' and 'no pressure or hard-sell'? Having pinpointed the crisis of age and infirmity, you need to leave your audience feeling good about the future.

Raise questions

The ubiquitous 'questions and answers' device is a simple and effective method of converting complex or unpalatable facts into user-friendly information.

Entire leaflets can be – and frequently are – written to this format, especially if a company wants to explain a change in familiar practice or usage to its customers. But Q & As can also be integrated into other pieces to mop up anything which hasn't been addressed in the main body copy.

Whether you apply the concept to a total project or single page, the advantage remains the same. You have the power to word your 'questions' in such a way that the 'answers' are a continuation of the sales process. Any journalists among you will recognise the parallel with political interviews: whatever you ask, the response always has a faint whiff of roses.

Here's how the device *might* be applied to our GentleRise Stairlifts test piece . . .

Test Piece

Project: 'Q & A' section for GentleRise Stairlifts magazine insert

Headline:

Any questions you'd like to raise?

Body copy:

Q: I live in a 600-year old haunted cottage and the staircase is very narrow and winding. Can you help?

A: Certainly. Our stairlifts are engineered by skilled craftsmen and designed to operate in homes of all ages. For extra confidence, we offer the option of a panic button link with Ghosthunters 'R' Us.

Q: What are the chances of my becoming stuck between floors and having to crawl the rest of the way?

A: Virtually none. GentleRise stairlifts have an extensive range of safety features to overcome difficulties like this. One of these is a built-in megaphone to enhance your shouts for help, should the need arise.

Q: Will I suffer any uncomfortable vibrations while using a GentleRise stairlift?

A: Not at all. In fact, most of our customers rather enjoy it.

Alright, so we had a bit of fun with this one. But you can see how useful a Q & A can be in appearing to reassure the reader, while neatly wriggling out of any negative aspects of the proposition.

Questionnaires are another popular marketing device, although their function is quite different from a Q & A. This is the way companies find out more about your buying habits, your lifestyle, your likes and dislikes. In its simplest form, a questionnaire can take the guise of a coupon added to an advertisement or leaflet prompting readers to request more information or place an order to buy. Anything included on the coupon other than the essential details needed to respond to the request is designed to help the company know more about its customers.

A questionnaire sometimes masquerades under different guises, such as an application form to buy or join something. Don't misunderstand me: the form is quite genuine in helping you to do whatever you are seeking to do. It's just that a great deal more information about you is requested than strictly necessary for the purpose in hand. This might sound rather insidious, but its only intention is to help the company identify new audiences or product development opportunities.

Copywriters are unlikely to be asked to write application forms (although I have done so occasionally in the past). But questionnaires are a common marketing device which could easily turn up in a brief. If so, you will be told the purpose of the questionnaire and probably an indication of the sort of questions you should include.

Add an incentive

Greed is a great motivator, which is why so many companies entice their customers with offers of free gifts or low introductory prices.

If you are given a brief which includes an incentive of some sort, it deserves a prominent place in your creative thinking. But there are other motivational ploys you can adopt to increase the desire to buy. For instance:

- indicate snob value by referring to the 'limited' or 'exclusive' nature of your offer (it can always be 'extended' at a later date if the ploy fails)

- increase its appeal by emphasising how many customers are already using and benefiting from your offer ('are you missing out?')
- worry them into a decision ('act now – tomorrow may be too late')
- emphasise any 'free' features of the offer ('call our free helpline', 'send for your free information pack' etc)
- leave them with something to think about ('last month, we paid out £2m in benefits to our members')

You can also make very good use of outer and inner envelopes as an incentive to open up, read on and act. Charity appeals are a classic example, where emotive messages on the front are often accompanied by pictures of sad or hungry children, frail pensioners, victims of natural disasters, or anything else related to the subject of the appeal. Having been moved to open the pack, the recipient will find a pre-paid, ready addressed envelope inside to encourage a speedy and easily sent donation.

The strategy of using a two-step envelope incentive is used exhaustively for postal advertising and marketing. Check the next influx of mail on your doorstep for a wide variety of working examples. Some envelopes are used as sales devices in their own right. Remember the infamous bangtails from Chapter 4? If you are on the *Reader's Digest* mailing list (and who isn't), or belong to a postal membership service such as a book or record club, you are undoubtedly besieged by bangtails every month. These are the cunning little chaps which pose as a reply envelope for your order but include a tempting additional offer which you have to tear off before the envelope can be sealed.

Any device which involves the audience in having to take physical action of some sort (other than tearing it up and depositing it in the bin) is deemed to be a success. And bangtails are remarkably successful.

From me to you: saying it in a letter

Letters can turn up more frequently in a copywriting brief than almost any other kind of job. Companies use them extensively, both as sales devices in their own right and as accompaniments to others.

The great value of letters is that they personalise an advertising or marketing proposition in a way that no other method can match. Databases can, of course, be used to insert personal details about customers into a wide variety of other materials, but it never quite comes off. We aren't fooled by the device because that's exactly what it looks like: a device.

Letters are different. They are cheaper to produce for a start, so companies can afford to use bang-up-to-the-minute information about their customers to increase the impression of a personal communication directed solely at them – for instance:

- 'I know you are already using and enjoying brand X, so I wanted you to be the first to hear some exciting news . . . '

- 'Now that your new business is up and running, this could be a great time to add brand X as a complement to brands Y and Z . . . '

- 'You don't need us to tell you how much extra work a baby can create, but brand X is something you will *both* welcome into your lives . . . '

A letter can be used for many more purposes than simple sales devices like these. To entice lost customers back into the fold, for example, or remind them to renew a membership. They can act as appetite-whetters by heralding good news to come; damage-limitation exercises following bad publicity; even as congratulations for special events or achievements linked to the relationship between company and customer.

There's no particular 'set format' for letters. They can be a matter of two or three paragraphs in length or run to an equivalent number of pages; range from standard A4 or A5 to virtually any size or shape you wish (or, more accurately, the budget allows). As always, the brief is your starting point for planning and writing letters.

Let's return to GentleRise Stairlifts (seriously this time) and take two quite different examples of using letters as a marketing device.

Test Piece (1)

Project: Follow-up customer enquiry letter for GentleRise Stairlifts

Dear Mr. Jones,

Great news – you can now save <u>twice as much</u> on a GentleRise Stairlift!

I know you are just back from hospital, so here's some really great news to welcome you home.

You are one of an exclusive number of customers who can now take advantage of a very special saving on GentleRise Stairlifts. Because of your recent hip operation, you are eligible for <u>twice our standard introductory discount</u> – that's **20%** instead of the 10% we told you about before.

We're here to ease your worries as well as your mobility
I'm sure you have a hundred questions to ask about installing a GentleRise Stairlift – such as:

- can it accommodate that awkward bend in my staircase?
- is there much upheaval while it is fitted?
- will it spoil the look of my home?

It's only natural to be concerned that everything runs smoothly, in every sense of the phrase. Our sympathetic and experienced advisers can answer all your questions and will be happy to show you a video or photographs of GentleRise Stairlifts in action. You can then see for your-self how easily they accommodate the most challenging stairways with the minimum of fuss or disturbance.

It only takes a phonecall – at our expense, of course
Can we make a date to visit you? I promise you will be put under no pressure to buy. All we want is to give you the facts so that you can make an informed decision about whether a GentleRise Stairlift is right for you.

You can call us any time, day or night. We'll pay for the call. In the meanwhile, please accept our very best wishes for a speedy recovery.

Yours sincerely,

P.S. As you'll appreciate, this terrific saving can't last forever so do call us as soon as you can. To save you looking it up, our 24-hour freephone helpline number is **0800 123456**.

Test Piece (2)

Project: GentleRise Stairlifts damage-limitation letter following adverse TV documentary

Dear Mr. Jones,

I can well understand how anxious you must be after the recent television documentary about collapsing stairlifts.

Let me reassure you immediately that GentleRise is in no way connected with the manufacturers featured on the programme and that your stairlift complies in every detail with published safety standards. We have already taken issue with the programme makers about the needless worry they have caused our customers and they have promised to broadcast a retraction.

I sincerely hope that this irresponsible programme will in no way spoil the freedom and convenience of using your GentleRise Stairlift.

However, to show how seriously we take our customers' safety and peace of mind, we have set up a free telephone advice line for you to call if you are still worried in any way. The number is **0800 678910** and it will be open for the next 14 days.

With all good wishes,

Yours sincerely,

Analysis
Both letters adopt a one-to-one approach from writer to reader, but the structure and tone of voice differ considerably from one to the other.

Test piece (1) is designed to sell, pure and simple, so the AIDA principle is strongly in evidence. It captures attention in the opening seconds with a headline identifying a clear benefit for Mr. Jones: the opportunity to save money. The offer is underlined to increase impact. Momentum is maintained by leading straight into a knowledgeable message about the customer's recent operation (information garnered from his original request for details about the stairlifts).

Interest and desire start to build as Mr. Jones learns more about the offer – again using underlining for emphasis – and that he is one of only a few customers who can benefit from it. The information is broken up into readable chunks by using a second heading followed by a bullet-pointed list of typical customer concerns, all of which can be assuaged by the company's 'sympathetic and experienced advisers'.

Finally, the call to action is heralded by a third headline emphasising the cost-free nature of contacting the company. This is reinforced by a postscript urging speedy action and reminding him of the number to call.

Test piece (2) is designed to fulfil a very different function. Mr. Jones, having bought his stairlift, has now been subjected to a worrying TV exposé about the risk of it collapsing while in use. GentleRise's reputation is at stake, not to mention the danger of customers demanding that the goods be removed and a refund given.

This time, there are no eye-catching headlines and the tone of voice is authoritative and grave. The letter is short and to the point but not abrupt. It retains the sincerity of a me-to-you approach but in the context of two people combined against a common enemy.

Although the way you structure and compose letters will, as our two examples show, vary according to the objectives you've been set, you may find the following suggestions helpful as a general guideline:

- bring in the 'you' factor as early as possible, preferably in the opening sentence or headline
- get to the main point of your letter quickly
- use clear, simple language and short sentences
- break the copy up with paragraphs, sub-headings or bullet points
- use underlining to increase impact
- if a response is called for, make it easy for the reader to do so
- make use of a PS to reinforce a key benefit or urge a call to action

107

Revisions, redrafts and yet more redrafts

Because I enjoy being a copywriter as much as I do, it's difficult not to be enthusiastic about the subject. But there is one aspect of the job that's tedious at best and soul-destroying at worst.

No matter how carefully you craft your work, it *will* be changed by others. Invariably many times over. And there is very little you can do about it other than take rearguard action early on to ensure you don't increase the number of redrafts unnecessarily.

Murdering your darlings

One of the ways you can minimise the amount of blood on the carpet (or red ink on the page) is to murder your darlings your-self before somebody else gets to them.

Have you indulged in words, phrases or headlines that you absolutely love but know in your heart will raise (or lower) eye-brows in other quarters? It probably isn't worth keeping them, unless you feel really strongly about it (see 'Defence and defeat').

Are there any areas where you can cut back on the number of words? Perhaps by converting a sentence into bullet points to give it more impact?

Do consecutive sentences or paragraphs start with the same word? Even a repeated 'the' can make copy look tedious.

Other than prepositions and conjunctions, have you used the same word twice in close succession? An 'impressive' offer, for example, which goes on to list an 'impressive' range of benefits.

Are you making bold claims about your subject that will never get past the client's legal department? If so, try softening 'will' to 'could' or 'can' to 'should' – e.g 'brand X *could* help you look younger' or 'you *should* lose unsightly wrinkles overnight' (I wish).

Finally – and obviously – have you run the spell-checker over your work to pick up errors and double-checked uncertainties in the dictionary? Are there commas where there should be full stops, and vice versa? Could any words be misconstrued, or better ones used?

As I said earlier, it won't necessarily cut down on the number of redrafts you have to write. But at least you'll have done your best.

Have you answered the brief?

Back to our old friend again. There really is no point in sub-mitting concepts or copy if they don't do what the brief asks them to do.

Whatever task you are tackling, always check back as you go – and especially when you finish – to make sure that every point in the brief is covered. Have you missed any USPs? Is the propo-sition clearly laid out? If you have taken an unusual approach to the subject, have you included a 'safe' alternative? Do you need to attribute any facts you've quoted? Is the call to action correct?

No matter how well-written or creative your approach might be, if it doesn't answer the brief, it doesn't do the job.

Accepting justifiable criticisms

Copywriting, as I've said many times, has a number of parallels with other areas of writing. One of them is that someone else is usually the best judge of your work. You have been living with it for hours, days or weeks, but they are seeing it for the first time.

This book, for instance, was read heroically at every stage of writing by a close friend and colleague who pounced on oddities, confusions, nonsenses and no-nos. His criticisms were, in almost every case, entirely justified. Even on the rare occasions when I disagreed with his comments, it still made me pause long enough to see if there wasn't a better way of phrasing some-thing, or a more appropriate example to include.

So it will be when you write copy. Another person can spot weaknesses far more easily than you because they haven't been up half the night battling with elusive words or impossible deadlines.

Resisting ticklers

To paraphrase Malvolio in *Twelfth Night*, some copy is born great, some achieves greatness and some has clients thrust upon it.

There will be times, many of them, when you come up against people who simply can't resist tickling your copy. A word here, a phrase there, a convoluted sentence somewhere else. It does nothing to improve what was there originally, but the temptation to tickle around with it proved irresistible.

It can be infuriating, but there is often little you can do about it other than grit your teeth and try to reach a compromise.

Defence and defeat

If you genuinely believe that something you have written is right or necessary and somebody else wants it taken out, you can and should defend it. Otherwise, it makes a nonsense of writing it in the first place. Put your arguments politely and explain why you believe the piece will suffer if this particular item of copy is omitted.

If it concerns a project you are writing on behalf of an agency and the account director agrees with you, he or she will usually defend it on your behalf. Alternatively, you may be asked to put your arguments to the client direct, either by phone or face to face.

There will be times when you win and others when you don't. If it's the latter, all you can do is accept defeat with as much equanimity as possible and move on to the next job. It isn't the end of the world, merely the end of that particular piece as a contender for your portfolio.

8. In Other Words . . . 'Plain English' Writing

Samuel Johnson defined 'net' as 'Anything reticulated or decussated at equal distances, with interstices between the intersections.' Had he produced this explanation today, he would undoubtedly have been in the running for a pound of tripe and a Golden Bull award from the Plain English Campaign.

This chapter is, in many ways, a celebration of the PEC's work and the tireless determination of its founder, Chrissie Maher, to stamp out what she calls utter drivel (a book listing many of the worst examples has been published under that title by the Campaign). I am indebted to Chrissie and her team for allowing me to draw on their materials, many of which have reduced me – and the writers' groups I address – to tears of laughter. But most of all, I am grateful for all the extra work that has come my way as a result of PEC's pressure on businesses to word official documents in language that people can read and understand.

Anyone who has ever taken out an insurance plan, bank loan, pension or mortgage will know how quickly materials change once the money is handed over. All those friendly, encouraging advertisements and sales leaflets – written, of course, by professionals like us – give way to terrifying documents listing parties of the first part doing incomprehensible things to parties of the second.

And it isn't only legal documents which set out to baffle and bewilder. The next few pages draw on dozens of examples of gobbledygook taken from PEC files which range from memos about hospital beds to theories about God. But the worst culprits are the businesses which take your money then confuse you to such an extent that you can get little benefit from your investment. Thanks to Chrissie Maher, most are now rapidly reviewing their literature – and good writers can capitalise on the opportunities this offers.

Crystal clear?

The Plain English Campaign was launched in 1979, although its roots go back to Chrissie Maher's childhood. Unable to read and write until she was in her mid-teens, Chrissie's first battle with officialdom was over the convoluted wording of Government welfare benefit forms. When she realised that friends with better educational advantages than she were also struggling to understand and fill in the forms, Chrissie decided the time had come to do something about it.

She set up camp opposite the Houses of Parliament and started to shred hundreds of incomprehensible government forms. When the police arrived on the scene, they proved her point admirably by reading out a 100-word sentence from the 1839 Metropolitan Police Act. Chrissie heard them out, then asked sweetly: 'Does that gobbledygook mean we have to clear off?'

Since then, this redoubtable Liverpudlian has taken on government departments, banks, building societies, insurance companies, hospitals, railways, the utilities and countless other lovers of legalese and shamed them into submission. The much-prized Crystal Mark is awarded to those who write to the Campaign's standards – and the tripe and bull to those who don't.

Top marks in the latter category go to an NHS staff circular which used 160 words to define a hospital bed. Here's an extract:

> A device or arrangement that may be used to permit a patient to lie down when the need to do so is a consequence of the patient's condition rather than a need for active intervention such as examination, diagnostic intervention, manipulative treatment, obstetric delivery or transport.

Sharing the billing – if only for the cheek of describing it as 'clarified' – is British Rail's explanation of refunds for unexpired season tickets, which were 'not pro rata but . . . the difference, if any, between: i) the price paid for the season ticket and ii) the total cost of the appropriate combination of monthly and weekly, seven-day or five-day season tickets and full-return tickets necessary to cover one return journey per day up to the date the season ticket was handed in, less an administrative charge.'

It isn't only official documents which have that 'excuse me, can you say that again?' effect. Manufacturers of household goods are no less attached to writing convoluted claptrap to baffle their buyers. Examples include washing instructions with the advice to 'employ tepid water to eliminate the residues of soap or detergent' (i.e. rinse). Then there's the electric drill part described as having a 'major aspiration capacity for particular working exigencies'. No translation was available for this one – any offers?

Other examples cited by PEC include: 'If there are any points of which you require explanation or further particulars we shall be glad to furnish such additional details as may be required by telephone' (if you have any questions, please ring). And, less amusingly, 'the aircraft suffered an involuntary conversion' (the plane crashed).

How many of these would you recognise for their true meaning?

- 'non-multicolour capability' (black and white television)
- 'sunshine units' (nuclear radiation plants)
- 'localised capacity deficiency' (traffic jam)
- 'staggered green man facility' (road-crossing)
- 'pre-enjoyed vehicle' (used car)
- 'visitor uplift facility' (mountain cable car)
- 'grain-consuming units' (pigs, sheep and cows)
- 'position incentivised' (on the bonus list)
- 'skill-mix adjustments' (redundancies)
- 'achieving a positive budget variance' (ditto)
- 'a pay equalisation concept' (a large pay rise for the boss)
- 'period of adjustment' (a recession)
- 'meaningful downturn' (ditto)
- 'a difficult exercise in labour relations' (a strike)

Or these, which have left everyone – including hardened members of PEC – utterly baffled:

'Due to reorganisation, the basement will be on the second floor, half the second floor will be on the first floor but half will remain on the second. First floor will move to the basement.'

113

'Since data is central to the issue of refined implementation guidance and legislation defers implementation, we believe it is advisable to examine the data that your organisation is assembling to preclude any such unintended effects.'

'The spiritual body means whatever is appropriate to whatever is the dimension that subsumes the dimension we know about and extends into the dimension which is God.'

Finally, I'm not sure whether PEC included the following quotation (which appeared in one of its *Campaign International* magazines as a footnote to an article by the First Parliamentary Counsel, Christopher Jenkins) with tongue in cheek or not. It gives every appearance of being a 'proper' footnote to Mr. Jenkins' article – but judge for yourselves:

'2. A later edition of the book *[Practical Legislation]* dated 1902 contains the following passage, which is as relevant today as it was then: 'Mr Justice Stephen said, speaking from his own experience: "I think that my late friend, Mr Mill, made a mistake upon the subject, probably because he was not accustomed to use language with that degree of precision which is essential to every one who has ever had, as I have had on many occasions, to draft Acts of Parliament, which, although they may be easy to understand, people continually try to misunderstand, and in which, therefore, it is not enough to attain a degree of precision which a person reading in good faith can understand; but it is necessary to attain, if possible, to a degree of precision which a person reading in bad faith cannot misunderstand. It is all the better if he cannot pretend to misunderstand it . . ."'

Understanding what's needed

It's only fair to redress the balance slightly by putting the legal point of view in perspective. Although there is no excuse for using deliberately complex or confusing language, many of the legal departments I have worked with in 'translating' documents into plain English are genuinely concerned that oversimplification can be dangerous.

Their argument is that a great many of the materials under fire from PEC are legal contracts between buyer and seller. If the 'rules' are not set out in a precise and detailed manner, they not only place the organisation at risk from a lawsuit but could also be viewed by ombudsmen and other watchdogs as an unfair contract.

Chrissie Maher sees it differently. In her words: 'Many lawyers still believe that plain language documents are "unsafe" but unlike traditionally-drafted legal documents, none of those that we have worked on have ever had to be presented in court for interpretation. Lawyers also fail to realise that there is much more to a plain language approach to producing law texts than simply getting rid of archaic legal language.'

Speaking as a copywriter who values the work – and the income – from companies who recognise the need for change but do not entirely agree with PEC's forthright approach, I have learned to be pragmatic.

My first attempt at converting a strangulated insurance policy into a user-friendly contract was met with great suspicion (and more than a little sarcasm) by the author of the document. Twelve drafts and some weeks later, we had both learned to respect the other's point of view. The final version was nowhere near Crystal Mark standards but it was a transformation from the original. And an education in every sense for me. I learned much about the workings of the legal mind and the reasons why so many seemingly unnecessary repetitions are considered to be indispensable by the profession.

I also discovered that, far from making documents shorter, the plain English route can sometimes double them in size. Why? Because there are certain legally watertight words and phrases – e.g. 'acute' medical conditions as opposed to 'chronic' in health insurance policies – that have no comparable single alternative. The only way round it is to add an everyday description alongside, or create a plain English glossary to explain what they mean.

Babies and bathwater

The thing to remember when cleaning up any kind of legalistic language is that you could throw something of value away in your enthusiasm, rather like the proverbial baby with the bathwater.

Let's revisit the seemingly farcical NHS bed definition. I don't intend to offer a plain English interpretation of the piece, largely because I can't afford to incur the wrath of Government lawyers if I get it wrong. But it would be a useful exercise to consider why the NHS felt it necessary to issue the definition in the first place. Why take 160 words to describe a hospital bed when most of us would use just two? The clue lies not so much in the wording of the piece as in the readers it was intended to reach. It appeared, if you remember, in an NHS staff circular, which means that it was aimed at doctors, nurses, hospital administrators etc, not at the general public. Why would these hard-working people be subjected to such an apparently meaningless tirade? Almost certainly because hospital beds are in permanently short supply and the occupation of each has to be justified. Note the phrase 'permit a patient to lie down'. What I think the piece is actually trying to say is that hospital beds are for rest and recuperation, not for operations, childbirth and the like.

But, of course, I could be wrong . . .

The point I am making is that you need to understand the 'what and why' of complex wording before you can arrive at a translation. Looking at some of the examples given in this chapter, you could be forgiven for abandoning the whole idea here and now. Yet there is a very simple way of working out what's meant by seemingly unintelligible prose: ask the perpetrator to explain it to you. Verbally, that is, *not* in writing.

Can it really be that easy? Yes, because whoever is asking you to tackle the project is paying good money for your time and effort. So there would be very little point in not giving you the help you need to do the job.

Step by step

One thing I can promise you is that you are highly unlikely to 'crack' a plain English project in one draft. The more complicated the document you are working on, the longer it will take to reword to everyone's satisfaction. And do note the reference to 'everyone'. This is a job which involves teams rather than individuals. A company's legal department is often the end of a long chain which starts with the people who developed the product, progresses through the quality controllers and then passes to the marketing specialists. It is the latter who are most likely to commission – and pay for – your services, although it is the legal experts who have the final say over whether your work is up to the mark. Not surprisingly, there is often considerable friction between these two departments. Marketing people have budgets to balance; their legal counterparts have lawsuits to consider. There's not much you can do about the politics of situations like this, other than to remain professional and get on with the job as best you can.

If you are working on the project through an agency – as opposed to writing direct for the company concerned – you will also be answerable to the account director, creative director and design team who have their own roles to play in the process. Either way, you will need to comply with agreed deadlines and copy budgets, both of which can be almost impossible to judge.

Given all of this, perhaps it isn't so surprising that legal documents have taken so long to work their way into the 20th century. Now all we have to do is get them through the millennium . . .

Stage by stage

In my experience, converting a document such as an insurance policy into plain English needs at least six stages.

• **STAGE ONE: getting to grips with the original.** You will be sent the document in question to assess how much work is involved and how long it is likely to take. Read it carefully and use a highlighter pen on complex or confusing sections to remind yourself which ones you need to query. If there are structural changes you would like to make, such as the running order of the document or the way legal definitions are set out, make a list so that you are armed with the right questions when discussing the project face to face. If possible, try and negotiate a first draft budget at this stage (for all the reasons given in the 'Step by step' section) and remember to allow for at least one meeting.

• **STAGE TWO: the initial discussion meeting.** This is when you get a chance to meet the person – or people – who drafted the original document and will be monitoring its rewording. You need to gain their trust and confidence in your ability to

117

do the job, so try not to be too critical of the current wording (however bad it is). Point out the areas of difficulty you have identified from your first reading and ask them to explain any that have beaten you. If you want to drop anything from the document, or reorganise the order in which the information is given, this is the time to say so. It may not be feasible, in which case you'll be wasting your time in trying. If possible, take a tape recorder along with you so that you don't have to spend the entire meeting scribbling notes.

- **STAGE THREE: preparing the first draft.** This takes considerable concentration, so try and clear your schedule of other jobs which will interrupt the flow. You may need to ring the legal team, or other people involved in the job, with questions or difficulties you hadn't spotted on the first reading. If so, wait until you can deal with several points in one call, rather than making frequent calls throughout the day. You are dealing with busy people who will lose patience if they have to stop what they are doing every two or three hours to take telephone calls.

- **STAGE FOUR: submitting the draft for approval.** If you are doing the job through an agency, you need to let the account director see the draft first before submitting it to the client. He or she will be a good barometer in testing how much easier the document is to read and understand and whether any sections need improvement. When you are both satisfied that nothing more can be done at this stage, several copies of the draft will be sent to the client for circulating to everyone involved in the approval process.

- **STAGE FIVE: initial reactions.** You may be asked to attend another meeting with the legal team to discuss/negotiate points of conflict or concern in the draft. If not, it will come back to you – either direct or via the agency – filled with comments, changes and suggestions. These may take the form of scribbled points on each page, or separate guidelines typed up by the various people involved. At worst, you will receive back every copy that was circulated, each with different and possibly conflicting comments, which you then have to co-ordinate as best you can. If in doubt, adopt changes suggested by the most senior members of the team and set others aside to query later.

- **STAGE SIX: preparing the second draft.** Although this can be frustrating in terms of seeing your carefully simplified wording subjected to legalese once again, it is an easier stage to work on than the original draft. The design team should get involved now, if they haven't already, because simplicity of layout is just as important as clarity of wording. Especially if the document is to stand any chance of gaining a coveted PEC Crystal Mark.

If all this sounds a little daunting, just think of the pride you can take in your work when the document finally goes to print. You have the satisfaction of knowing that, thanks to your efforts, somebody is going to understand exactly what they have bought, how to use it and what to do if anything goes wrong. Not a bad outcome.

Other aspects of plain English writing

PEC's work isn't only confined to legal and technical documents. The Campaign is also actively involved in simplifying business letters, reports and sales literature. Indeed, it runs a number of courses for just that purpose, both 'open' and 'in-house'.

As a professional working copywriter, I am entirely in agreement that clear, simple language is essential. However, I have to say that PEC's enthusiasm for short sentences and plain words can sometimes make for a rather 'flat' approach. My role – and yours if you take up the challenge of this book – is to enthuse a target audience into making a decision of some kind. That's what copywriters are paid to do. Over-simplified wording and over-short sentences can take the fire out of the message.

Here's an extract from one of PEC's own sales leaflets, which is promoting a relatively expensive diploma course. Judge for yourselves.

About the Plain English Campaign Diploma
Since Plain English Campaign began in 1979, we have been offering courses in plain English. These courses give people an excellent grounding in plain English techniques. We have developed the Diploma Course to give people a higher level

of expertise. It helps to have a qualification in plain English if you are trying to persuade other people in your organisation to write clearly.

How will it help your organisation?
By using plain English you will save your organisation time and money. You will be more efficient and save time when you write. Your customers will understand what you are trying to tell them first time. Staff will not spend endless hours on the phone sorting out misunderstandings, or answering questions that should have been dealt with in letters.

Your customers will think more highly of you. They will realise that you care about them and have their interests in mind.

In my view, this has been simplified to death. There's no spark to fire the imagination, no reason to respond. But that is a personal view and you might disagree entirely.

Useful publications from PEC

Having dealt with the only criticism I have about the Campaign's work, let me end as I started – with unconditional praise. PEC has an impressive list of books and leaflets, many of which now have a permanent place of honour on my desk. They are very reasonably priced and sent to you within a day or so of ordering.

Here is a list of the publications available as I write, complete with shortened versions of the descriptions provided by PEC.

- *The Plain English Story*
  A book describing how the Campaign grew from an advice agency in Salford into an organisation that is regularly consulted by the UK's largest companies.

- *A–Z of alternative words*
  This useful guide lists hundreds of words that make writing dull, confusing and long-winded and gives plain English alternatives.

- *A-Z guide to legal words*
  Designed to help members of the public translate legal jargon into plain English.

- *A-Z of legal words and phrases*
  Designed to help solicitors explain legal wording to clients in plain English. It also includes translations of some Latin and Norman French words and phrases.

- *Plain English Campaign mouse mat*
  Complete with guidelines on using plain English.

- *Utter Drivel*
  PEC's second collection of gobbledygook. The book contains a mind-boggling array of public information and public statements that makes hilarious, if bewildering, reading. It also offers valuable tips on how to write good plain English.

- *How to write letters in plain English/How to write reports in plain English*
  Two 'DIY' courses which explain the techniques of clear writing, backed up by progressively more difficult exercises. Each book contains suggested answers and each course takes about six hours to complete.

- *Language on Trial – The Plain English Guide to Legal Writing*
  This book will interest anyone who has had experience of the language of the law. In particular, it will be a valuable aid for lawyers involved in drafting legal documents or wanting to communicate clearly with clients and colleagues. The final chapter offers over 30 pages of guidance and practice in writing plain English, which will be of use to anyone whose job involves putting pen to paper.

- *Special offer pack*
  Utter Drivel, Plain English Story, mouse mat, one A-Z guide and one DIY course.

- *Plain English Magazine*
  Produced three or four times a year and available free to anyone who asks for their name to be put on the mailing list.

For information about current prices, or to place an order, write, phone or fax Plain English Campaign at: PO Box 3, New Mills, High Peak, SK22 4QP. Phone: 01663 744409. Fax: 01663 747038.

9. Getting in the Money

There's very little point in sweating over a hot brief if you don't get paid for it. And as the money won't roll in until you roll out an invoice, this chapter is all about the business end of freelance copywriting.

Which means it's also about **you**. Freelancing is like no other kind of business because the service you provide is personal in every sense of the word. It's your skill and originality that clients are buying, so you need to put a value on yourself as well as on your work. Especially given the notoriously stressful nature of the advertising and marketing industry.

Most copywriters would agree that a measure of stress isn't necessarily bad from the creative angle: looming deadlines can focus the mind wonderfully. But there's a difference between being challenged and writing yourself ragged.

Conversely, there will be times when there isn't much work around, so it's important to plan for this and keep things in perspective. The summer months are often relatively quiet for the obvious reason that clients are away on holiday. That's the time to do your Christmas shopping because it's a virtual certainty you won't have another opportunity in the hectic pre-season rush of work. Yet even these two regular lows and highs can change gear occasionally and you could (as I have) find yourself in the midst of a frenetically busy August or frighteningly quiet December.

You could even find yourself busiest of all when times are lean for everyone else. The advertising and marketing industry is often seen as an economic barometer: if agency budgets are cut back, the indication is that businesses are experiencing a chilly front. But if they don't advertise or market their wares, how can they warm up their customers and insulate their profits? The answer is to seek out a more economic way of maintaining their public profile – and that can be very good news for freelances.

To establish yourself on the freelance scene, your services need to be competitively priced as well as skilful. So it's important to set the right value on those skills.

How to set fees for your work

Unlike most other freelance writers, copywriters set their own fees rather than working within pre-set payment structures.

This might sound like a licence to print money, but there are pitfalls. If you quote too high a fee, you not only risk pricing yourself out of that particular project but also any future work from the same source. Equally, if you put too low a value on your work, clients may be wary about your ability and professionalism.

The alternative is to ask clients if they have a budget in mind for the job. This has the advantage of saving you the headache of working out a reasonable fee and could be welcomed by agencies, who have their own mark-ups to add to your costs. Don't begrudge them their percentage because they do all the work in getting the brief – and usually work equally hard to 'sell' your copy to the client.

But you need to have a rough idea in mind of what the job deserves before accepting a proffered fee. If you feel it's worth more than the suggested figure, don't be afraid to say so. The worst that can happen is a refusal, but negotiation is far more likely. If they want you for the job, they could be prepared to pay a little more to get you.

Do be wary of clients who promise loads of extra work if you agree to a low initial fee. There's a surprising number of amnesiacs out there.

Charging hourly or daily rates

A good starting point for working out a realistic fee is to base it on an hourly or daily charging rate. Many agencies use the same basis for negotiating – and invoicing – their own client fees and will welcome the practicality of working with you in this way.

There are three methods you could use to arrive at a suitable charging rate.

1. Work it out on a 'need to' basis – need to eat, need to pay the mortgage, need to sleep, etc. – much as you would for a wage or salary.
2. Find out what other freelance copywriters in your area are charging (a few telephone calls posing as a client is a sneaky but effective method).
3. Ask the agency or company you are approaching if they already use freelances and what rates they currently pay.

The most practical method is to use all three in that order. Working out the amount you need for survival is an obvious place to start, but you also have to be competitive. That's where points (2) and (3) can be a reassuring back-up in confirming that your sums are on track.

Converting an hourly rate to a daily rate is simply a matter of multiplying the first by the second. I work on the basis of an 8-hour day, which saves having to mess around with odd half-hours, so my daily rate is eight times my hourly one. Once you've decided what your charging rate will be, you then need to work out how many hours (or days) a job will take to complete. For example:

- how complicated is it?
- how good a brief do you have?
- how much information is available?
- how many meetings will be involved?
- are you quoting for a first draft or finished job?

Estimating a realistic fee in advance is far from a definite science, because the only way to discover how long a job will take is to do it. Even with experience, you can easily miscalculate.

Always be prepared to think again if clients come over faint at your first suggestion. On the other hand, if they accept your quote swiftly, you may have underestimated the job and they can't believe their luck.

Charging on a 'per project' basis

This is a natural progression from charging by the hour or day. The only difference is that you quote for the type of job involved e.g. a press release, a 2-page letter, an 8-page brochure, and so on.

It's more common to charge on a per project basis when freelancing for a company than an agency, although you could be asked to do so by either. The best method is to use a price range rather than trying to arrive at a finite sum – 'press releases from £xx to £xx', for instance. This can be worked out by deciding the minimum and maximum amount of time a project might take, then multiplying by your hourly charging rate.

Some jobs could have quite a wide price range. Our working example shows how something relatively straightforward like a press release can vary enormously in the amount of time one can take over another. I have shown the thinking process behind the calculations; it could be helpful if you do the same when explaining to clients what they might have to pay, and why.

Working Example

Calculating a price range for press releases

Least complicated/minimum time input – e.g:
- briefed by phone
- straightforward news message
- no interviews necessary
- faxed direct to client or news editor
- likely writing time 4 hours

Lower price range: 4 x £xx hourly charging rate

Most complicated/maximum time input – e.g:
- attending pre-launch product briefing
- creating a good news angle
- conducting interviews
- liaising with editors and news desks
- likely writing/preparation time 12 hours

Upper price range: 12 x £xx hourly charging rate

If the projects you are pricing need design input as well as copywriting (leaflets and brochures, for example), remember to add time for creative briefings and liaison with the designers. And emphasise that your fee is for copywriting only. If the client wants you to quote a total price for a finished item, you will need to cultivate the services of good local designers, artworkers and printers, all of whose costs must be taken into account.

Dealing with purchase orders and job numbers

Just as you quote other people's references when replying to business correspondence, so you do with purchase orders and job numbers.

These are the methods by which clients can cross-reference your fee to the project concerned. You are, technically, a supplier and businesses may want evidence that your services were ordered and paid for. I say 'technically' because freelance copywriters – together with freelance designers, photographers, illustrators and all the other skilled professionals who contribute to the creative process – tend to be looked on as part of the team rather than faceless outsiders.

Nonetheless, we are not on the payroll so our charges are justifiable expenses for clients to offset against their own.

The difference between purchase orders and job numbers is self-explanatory. The first relates to buying your services and the second to the project for which they were commissioned. Both references need to be quoted on your invoice. If not, the financial director (or whoever else is responsible for paying it) cannot relate your work to their records and your cheque could either be held back or not paid at all.

It isn't mandatory for clients to issue purchase orders or job numbers. Many are quite happy to commission your services without providing either. As long as you relate your invoice clearly to the work you have done, that's all they will require of you.

Working Example

XYZ Limited – Purchase Order No. 12345

(please quote the above number on all related invoices)

<u>To:</u>   A. Goode, Freelance Copywriter

<u>Date:</u> 31.12.1999

<u>Re:</u>   Job No. 678 – Client reference ABC

<u>Please supply:</u>

First draft copy for 12-page ABC product brochure.

<u>Agreed budget:</u>   16 hours

<u>Required by:</u>   4.1.2000

<u>Signed:</u>   *A. Director*

Sending invoices and statements

Whether or not you are given a purchase order or job number, you will always have to send out an invoice. And very probably follow it up with at least one statement.

The important thing to include on both (apart from your fee) is the date you expect to be paid. Note the word 'expect' rather than 'hope'. This is something you need to sort out with clients, preferably at the start of your working relationship together. Some organisations take a disgracefully long time to settle invoices, even if they relate to work which has increased both their customers and their profits. This reluctance to pay is insidious and could affect you whether you are writing direct for the organisation concerned or one of its agencies.

Successive governments have tried to do something about slow payers with very little success. Your best means of avoiding them is to ask new clients what their policy is for settling invoices. A month or less is reasonable; anything longer is not. Remember that you will have invested a considerable amount of time in the job already when the invoice is sent. Why should you have to spend more waiting for it to be paid?

Unfortunately, whatever steps you take to protect yourself, practices like this can and will affect you from time to time. And there is an additional element of uncertainty about freelancing. You have to take clients on trust because very few will be prepared to pay for your work in advance. Some, regrettably, may renege on the deal altogether. The small claims section of the County Court is an obvious recourse if you come up against such a situation, but you may find it difficult to prove your case if your work hasn't been used for any reason.

This isn't intended to alarm you, merely to make you aware of the realities of working for yourself and encourage you to take sensible precautions. In fifteen years or so of freelancing, I have only had two bad debts, both from companies which went out of business through very little fault of their own.

All you can do about setting the rules for payment is to make your position quite clear from the outset. Specify when you expect your invoice to be settled: within 15 or 30 days, for instance. But be reasonable – and realistic – about how literally this is applied. Many companies have a 'cheque run' at the end of the month and won't take kindly to you insisting on a different payment date.

Having dealt with the bad guys, now for the good. Most reputable companies will settle your invoice as agreed within the time requested. Some may ask you to send a statement to remind them. A few might need you to jog their memories and cheque books a second time before settling up (rather like a red reminder).

Here are some working examples of invoice and statement layouts. The first is a follow-up to our previous purchase order example so that you can see the cross-referencing. The statement examples show progressive reminders, the first friendly and informal, the second slightly less so. Note that the requested payment date is shown large and clear on all the examples, together with the name in which the cheque should be made out.

Working Example (1)

A. Goode, Freelance Copywriter,

Anystreet, Anytown, AB12 3CD. Tel/Fax: 01234 567891

COPYWRITING INVOICE 4.1.2000

Order No.	Job No.	Client	Project	No. of hours
12345	678	ABC	Brochure	16

Total fee @ £xx per hour ££££

Agreed payment date: 31.1.2000

Please make cheques payable to 'A. Goode'

Working Example (2)
A. Goode, Freelance Copywriter,
Anystreet, Anytown, AB12 3CD. Tel/Fax: 01234 567891
<u>COPYWRITING INVOICE: ABC BROCHURE 4.1.2000</u>
Professional charges for initial briefing meeting, creative
liaison, initial concepts and first draft copy.
Fee: <u>££££</u>

Agreed payment date: 31.1.2000
Please make cheques payable to 'A. Goode'

Working Example (3)
A. Goode, Freelance Copywriter,
Anystreet, Anytown, AB12 3CD. Tel/Fax: 01234 567891
Just a friendly reminder . . .

<u>Invoice Date</u>	<u>Job/Purchase No.</u>	<u>Project</u>	<u>Fee due</u>
4.1.2000	678/12345	Brochure	££££

in case this had slipped your mind!
Please make cheques payable to 'A. Goode'

Working Example (4)
A. Goode, Freelance Copywriter,
Anystreet, Anytown, AB12 3CD Tel/Fax: 01234 567891
<u>STATEMENT (SECOND REMINDER)</u>

<u>Reference:</u>	ABC product brochure
<u>Invoice date:</u>	4.1.2000
<u>Agreed fee:</u>	££££
<u>Agreed payment date:</u>	31.1.2000

PLEASE PAY NOW. CHEQUES PAYABLE TO 'A. GOODE'

Chasing money is always awkward, especially if you want to maintain a relationship with the people concerned. However, if a payment remains elusive, it's perfectly reasonable to telephone the company and ask why. There could be a good reason for it – staff illness or holiday absences for example.

If you find yourself having to chase them on a regular basis, it might be worth asking yourself if the time wouldn't be better spent in pursuing a new source of work.

Claiming expenses

Agencies are usually quite happy for you to claim travel costs and other related expenses if you are meeting clients on their behalf. These are then passed on to the client when the job is invoiced. But you shouldn't assume you will be reimbursed. Always ask for their policy on expenses before investing your hard-earned cash in rail fares, petrol or meals en route. If they aren't prepared to reimburse you, you could consider increasing your fee by an hour or so to cover the costs.

The latter method is also better if you are writing for a company. They can't pass your expenses on in the way an agency can and may balk at a list of additional costs on your invoice.

A less tangible expense than meals and travel is the cost of your time in relation to both. Copywriting fees are based on your creative and language skills, but as you won't be applying either (in the written sense) while en route to or from a meeting, what – if anything – should you charge? This is a tricky one to balance. Clients could be justified in resenting your meter running on full if you haven't yet started the job. From your perspective, the time you spend at their request in a meeting is preventing you from working on something else.

The fairest compromise is to agree on a reduced meeting and travel rate. It's in your interests to do so, because client briefings are an integral part of the job. If you prove too expensive to include in any of the discussions, it could put you at a disadvantage when you come to do the work. Worse still, the client may decide to look for another copywriter who is more inclined to be reasonable.

Making decisions about whether you should or shouldn't charge for meetings and by how much is largely a matter of common sense. If, as I do, you freelance regularly for one agency, it would be professional suicide to charge them every time they call you in for a job brief or to discuss a creative strategy. Equally, a new client who asks you to drop by to talk about a possible working relationship is hardly likely to be impressed if you whack in a bill for your time.

Look on situations like this as an investment. If they don't pay off, the most you have lost is a few hours out of your day.

Sorting out tax, VAT and insurance

A friend who has freelanced for many years called me recently, thoroughly shaken, to say that he owes several thousand pounds in back National Insurance contributions. It transpired that he had been paying the Class 4 contributions shown on his income tax demands every year, but not the weekly Class 2 contributions that sole traders and partners are also required to pay. The omission was finally picked up by his accountant from bank statements sent in for his annual accounts audit.

Some years ago, I suffered a similar fate over VAT. Having decided not to register because of the extra paperwork, I failed to notice that my earnings had crept over the threshold for compulsory registration. Again, it took an accountant to spot the oversight, but Customs and Excise were swift to exact punishment and I had to pay a hefty fine as well as the VAT they calculated I should have been charging my clients.

Neither my friend nor I could do anything about these oversights other than grit our teeth and find the money. In each case, our pleas for clemency were met with a steely 'ignorance of the law is no excuse'.

If you are going into freelance work, you need a working knowledge of what the law requires of sole traders and the self-employed. And you really need an accountant, as well. They may be expensive, but they pay for themselves in the long run and their fees can be offset against your tax bills. Apart from spotting costly mistakes and saving you from paying more than absolutely necessary to the tax man, they also save you time. And your time is valuable. Given the choice of earning good money from my writing skills or spending endless hours negotiating with the Inland Revenue, I know which I prefer. Much better to concentrate on doing what you do best and let your accountant do the same.

I am not going to attempt to go into the intricacies of tax, VAT and insurance in this book. There are plenty of others on the subject by people qualified to write them. One of the best is the *Lloyds Bank Small Business Guide* by Sara Williams (published by Penguin). It isn't cheap – my 1997 edition was £16.00 – but it is regularly recommended as a 'best buy' and given away free if you open a Lloyds Bank business account. Some of what it contains isn't relevant to freelancing (one chapter, for instance, deals with franchising and buying 'off the peg' businesses), but there's a lot of good stuff in there as well. See if you can find a copy in the library first before laying out the cash.

The only other recommendation I would make is to find a first-rate savings account and squirrel money into it on a regular basis. Bearing in mind what I said at the start of this chapter about being kind to yourself and planning for fluctuations in work and earnings, there's nothing quite like spare money for a comfort blanket. You also have to plan for unpleasant things like tax bills, National Insurance and VAT bills if you decide (or are obliged) to register.

Postal savings accounts usually offer the best interest rates and most will process cheque withdrawals by return of post. Some also offer plastic cards if you need the money in cash.

Building and maintaining good working relationships

I have always found it best to work with a few clients that I know really well rather than lots that I hardly know at all. It's easier to learn more about their customers, products or services that way. And my value increases because they don't have to run over old ground every time a new brief turns up.

This comforting sense of familiarity works both ways. It's much pleasanter to work regularly with people who become your friends than to be a perpetual outsider. Especially in an industry where shared ideas and experiences are essential to the thinking – and creative – process. The more you can prove yourself to be a reliable and likeable member of the team, the greater the likelihood they will call on your services again. And again.

The most important relationship in creative terms is the one between copywriter and designer. Larger advertising agencies invariably employ them as a team rather than individually, and that's exactly how they work and think. When you are freelancing, it is less easy to build a close partnership like this because you may have to work with several designers rather than one. And they, in turn, may have to work with other copywriters.

This strengthens my earlier argument that 'less is more' in terms of how many clients you have. There's a better opportunity to develop empathetic relationships with designers if you work together regularly on projects rather than once every few months.

Getting out of bad ones

Sadly, not every working relationship is as good as it might be. You could find yourself freelancing for clients whose attitude towards you and your work is cavalier at best and downright rude at worst. Examples include meetings regularly arranged and cancelled without warning. Permanently woolly briefs that take all your time and patience to sort out. Constant quibbles over your fees and endless weeks of chasing before they are paid.

This isn't a relationship. It's a nightmare. And the best way to deal with it is to wake up, get up and go.

Taking the initiative for more work

The better you get to know your clients, the easier it is to spot opportunities to increase your workflow. For example, one of my longest standing clients is a new homes developer. I write regular press releases and leaflets about their developments, as well as information sheets describing new benefits and services for their homebuyers.

As a result, I also look out for any interesting (or worrying) news on TV, the radio or in the press relating to the building or buying of new homes. Changing mortgage interest rates, for instance, or horror stories about cowboy builders. If I think there is an opportunity for my client to capitalise on these in some way, perhaps by issuing a press release about price discounts to offset a mortgage increase, or a leaflet highlighting the strict quality standards applied to all their developments, I call and suggest it. Very often, they welcome the suggestion and commission me to write the project.

Equally, if you are freelancing for an agency and receive an item through the post from a close competitor of their most valued client, a call to the account director could be useful. The chances are that both the agency and the client know about the competitor's activity, but it might prompt one or the other to suggest a retaliatory mailshot to show the client's product in an equally good (or better) light. Since you started the chain of thought, you are the natural choice to write the piece.

There may be times when the initiative comes from someone else and you are asked to work on a free or speculative basis as a result. This is relatively common with agencies, who are often asked to 'pitch' for work against others with only the promise of a tiny fee (or none at all) if they are unsuccessful. Even if they are not pitching for business in that sense, they could be exploring other opportunities to gain new clients or increase goodwill with an existing one.

Should you accept projects on a 'no win, no fee' basis? If it comes from a known and trusted source, yes. If the pitch is successful, you will almost certainly be commissioned to work on the full project and your time for the initial work could well be covered as well. But speculative work has obvious drawbacks and may have hidden dangers. Constant requests for freebies are not only unfair but could also indicate a degree of desperation. If so, your client may be in difficulties and it is time to re-examine your relationship.

Requests for speculative work from a potential new client are a tough call. Will a refusal impede the start of a valuable relationship . . . or are you being taken for a ride? There's no easy answer to this. All I would advise is that you treat such requests with great caution. And keep a careful watch to see if any work you provide on a speculative basis is subsequently used by the company. If so, you have every right to ask for payment.

Leaving yourself time to relax and unwind

This brings us back full circle to how the chapter began. Freelance copywriting is demanding, exciting, challenging and frequently exhausting. You will get creative blocks exactly the same as any other writer, but you still have to meet given deadlines. Even if it means working all through the night.

Given this kind of pressure, the risk of burn-out is obvious. If you don't give yourself a break, literally and figuratively, neither your health nor your career will last very long.

Try and reward yourself with a brief respite after a particularly stressful project, even if it's only a work-free weekend. Make the most of sunny days by taking the dog for a walk or having a half-hour laze in the garden. If you're feeling restless, pop down to the gym or round to a friend. Short breaks from the computer work wonders for creative thinking.

You have the potential to earn very good money, so spend it on a really great holiday once in a while. Especially if there's a lull in your workload and the alternative is to sit at home worrying about it.

What's the point of working hard if you can't occasionally play hard as well?

10. A Sample Campaign to Inspire You

In the course of this book, I have often recommended the words of aunt AIDA. As you are reading the final chapter, it proves that three of her principles have worked. Your **attention** has been caught, your **interest** aroused and your **desire** – steady on – is building.

Now for your call to **action**.

I can think of no better encouragement to start freelance copywriting than to end this book with a sample campaign . . . for *you*.

We are going to put theory into practice with one last test case. The difference with this one is that it continues throughout the chapter and takes you through every stage of planning, budgeting, developing and writing. Its purpose is to inspire you to launch a similar campaign for yourself by drawing on these and other techniques explored in the book.

The campaign strategy is seen from the viewpoint of a central character. Some of the 'tools of persuasion' described in Chapter 4 come into play – mailshots, inserts, press releases and others – so that you can see them in a practical working context. You will also share in the thinking process as ideas are developed or discarded.

A Goode test case

Meet Andrew Goode, a talented writer and the hero of our campaign. We came across him briefly in the last chapter when his name appeared on invoices and statements.

This tells us that Andrew has tackled a copywriting project already. It arose from a chance meeting with a freelance designer called Maria. She introduced him to one of her agency clients and they briefed him on a sales brochure to test his skills.

Andrew made a great success of it, but the agency is dragging its feet over paying his fee and he has decided to explore other options.

By way of additional background, Andrew has been a driving instructor for the past three years and runs his own business. He is familiar with changing work pressures, often finding himself with too many pupils or too few. Writing has always been a passion and Andrew writes regular articles and letters for the trade press, as well as press ads and leaflets to promote his driving school. He also writes and edits a newsletter for the local golf club, where he has been an enthusiastic member for ten years.

The agency project has opened Andrew's eyes to the exciting possibilities for freelance copywriting. He had no idea such an opportunity exists, having assumed that copywriters only work on prestigious TV and national press advertising campaigns.

First things first: the target audience

Andrew wants to build his confidence – and his portfolio – by approaching as sympathetic an audience as possible. As he runs a small business himself, it makes sense to target others of a similar ilk. He will have an affinity with his audience and an ability to talk their language.

Having read a number of A & C Black's *Writing Handbooks*, Andrew is familiar with the advice to 'write about what you know'. So he narrows his target audience down to independent driving schools and good local golf courses. These are businesses he knows well and can write about with authority.

To play safe, he narrows the field down further by targeting driving schools outside his immediate patch (in case he needs the safety net of driving tuition during lulls in copywriting).

As Andrew already has practical experience in writing advertising and marketing materials for his own business – plus his articles and newsletters – this seems to offer the best sales proposition. He can demonstrate to his audience that well-written materials work, because he has evidence to support his argument.

Feet on the ground: the campaign budget

Andrew is no Richard Branson and his budget is closer to tog sizes than telephone numbers. He needs a campaign strategy that will invest in his time and skills without damaging his pocket too badly.

As his success depends on building a personal rapport with his audience, Andrew decides to take a direct approach with a series of mailshots and door drops. His PC can cope with the letters, but what of the leaflets? If they are to carry any weight with his audience, professional design is essential.

He gives Maria a call and they agree to help each other out on a quid pro quo basis. She will design and print Andrew's sales literature on her Apple Mac for no more than the cost of materials. In return, Andrew will write some pieces to build Maria's portfolio. If either of them obtains work as a result, each will recommend the other to their respective clients.

Now Andrew is in a position to impress his audience with good quality marketing materials, all for the cost of paper, envelopes, stamps and a few phone calls to research contact names and addresses.

The next decision is advertising. Andrew's budget is fairly tight, so he limits himself to display ads in the local media and a slightly larger spread in the driving school and golfing trade press. He is offered a discount on leaflet inserts by two leading trade publications and takes them up on the offer.

Lastly, Andrew contacts all the editorial departments to ask about press releases. He's given some useful tips on how many words they normally accept and the deadlines to meet. This is encouraging. Free editorial will balance the money he has to find for advertising and inserts.

The campaign is beginning to take shape and the budget is on target. Andrew is now poised to attract his audience with:

- local and trade press ads
- leaflet inserts
- press editorial
- mailshots
- door drops

A hook to hang it on: the campaign theme

Having prepared his ground, Andrew turns to more creative matters. He wants a strong theme for his campaign: a hook to hang everything on, from advertising to editorial, letters to leaflets. Something his audience can identify with – and which will always be identified with him.

Perhaps the word-link between driving schools and golf driving ranges is the place to start – 'business drive' or 'driving home the advantage', for instance. But that makes no reference to copywriting. 'The drive for good copy?' Too obscure – Andrew's audience is unlikely to relate to the word 'copy'. 'Drive home the advantage with professionally written sales materials'? Too cumbersome.

Andrew switches to the obvious: the built-in bonus of his 'Goode' surname. 'A Goode drive for your business?' Again, no reference to copywriting. 'Goode writing in business'? Hmm. 'The word is Goode'? That might work. How about a Bond link? 'The word is Goode. Andrew Goode.' No, completely the wrong tone of voice for down-to-earth small businesses.

Maybe he's trying too hard. Why not keep it simple with the 'Goode word' campaign? That strikes the right note and has great potential for advertising and PR. 'Put in a Goode word for your business.' 'Local copywriter launches 'Goode word' initiative.' Yes, definitely.

Selling the need: product development

Although Andrew has decided on the type of copywriting service he wants to launch, he has to package it in a way that will demonstrate the benefits immediately. If not, he will have a tough job attracting attention to his proposition. And an even tougher one persuading his audience to buy into it.

What are the key benefits of his service and how do they meet the audience's needs? Andrew tries a 'so what?' approach.

- **Feature:** professionally written sales materials. *So what?*
- ***Benefit:*** *creates the right impression with your customers.*

- Feature: experienced local writer. *So what?*
- *Benefit: makes the service more personal and accessible.*

- Feature: wide range of options, including design and print. *So what?*
- *Benefit: complete flexibility to fit the product to your needs.*

- Feature: specialised knowledge of your business. *So what?*
- *Benefit: the confidence of using a writer who speaks your language.*

- Feature: less expensive than using agencies. *So what?*
- *Benefit: someone who understands the pressures on your budget.*

- Feature: fast, reliable service. *So what?*
- *Benefit: direct from me to you, on time – right first time.*

Six identifiable features and benefits. Is there some way of bringing these together to create a unique selling proposition?

Andrew has an idea. What if he takes a literal approach to packaging his services? He could develop a 'Goode word' sales and marketing kit with ready-to-use letters, mailshots, press ads, handouts and any other materials his customers need to promote their business.

The idea begins to take shape.

He calls Maria and they devise a simple but appealing outer wrapper for the kit. It requires a small initial outlay for materials but if the concept takes off, Andrew can buy in bulk and reduce production costs to a minimum. Some of the contents will also need Maria's input, so they agree a one-off fee for items involving design and print. Andrew knows he is spending money on a speculative basis, but the idea seems to have such potential that he's prepared to take the risk. He settles down to write the various pieces, drawing on his special knowledge of the driving school and golfing markets to make them relevant for his audience. Spaces are left so that businesses can personalise each item by adding logos, addresses, contact numbers, prices and other information.

The kit is ready, now for the marketing angle. Andrew wants his product to be flexible enough to meet the needs of a wide variety of businesses, from sole traders upwards. The best solution is a 'pick-and-mix' proposal: customers can choose as many or as few services as they want, with the option of adding more over time. This allows Andrew to put an attractive starting price on the kit: a major selling point, given his target market.

Now all he needs is a catchy name for the product: something to capture the attention and imagination of his audience. How about '**Goode words at the ready**'? Perfect. It reflects his campaign theme and puts a neat twist on the ready-to-use proposition.

The product is ready for marketing. But does it 'sell the need' to everyone in Andrew's target audience? Some of the larger driving schools or golf courses may prefer a more individual approach to their sales and marketing materials. Andrew decides to offer an alternative 'bespoke' service which will be priced individually, according to the nature of the task. He can add additional services such as newsletters and press releases to increase the appeal. A quick phonecall to Maria confirms that she is happy to work on commissioned projects whenever the need arises.

Andrew is ready to spread the Goode word . . .

Creating an impact: local and trade press advertising

Andrew has read about the AIDA principle and knows that his advertising must:

- attract the *attention* of his target audience
- arouse *interest* in his service
- build a *desire* to know more
- prompt *action* to enquire

Does 'Goode words at the ready' have headline impact? Or should he revert to the simplicity of the 'Goode word' campaign title? This offers a better opportunity to set the tone of voice – warm, friendly and approachable – but with an intriguing edge.

Can I put in a Goode word for your business?

Do you run a driving school or golf course? Are you ever stuck for words? 'Goode words at the ready' is the answer.

- Range of professionally written sales and marketing materials
- Choose as many or as few as you need
- Prices start from only £xx

Call Andrew Goode now for more details.

01234 567891

That works well for the local media display ad. But the trade press ads have to be targeted specifically at their audience.

Andrew reworks the local ad slightly and adds more detail to capitalise on the extra space available. The same copy can be used for each of the two trade versions; all it needs is a change of word here and there to make it relevant for the audience concerned.

Can I put in a Goode word for your [driving school] [golf course]?

Stuck for words when it comes to advertising and marketing? Looking for a low-cost, high impact service to do the job for you?

'Goode words at the ready' is the answer.

- Attract new [pupils] [members] with very little effort or outlay
- Professionally written mailshots, ads, sales letters and more
- Specialised knowledge of the [driving school] [golfing] market
- Ready to use – can be personalised with your name and logo
- Choose the items you need and can afford

- Prices start from only £xx
- Alternative 'written to order' service also available

Call Andrew Goode now for more details.

01234 567891

Keeping up the momentum: trade press inserts

Andrew can't afford to be too ambitious, so he settles for a simple 4-page A5 leaflet for the inserts. Their primary task is to support his advertising, but another 'intriguing' headline (or the same one) would be too much. A direct approach is better. Again, Andrew develops a basic copy approach for both leaflets with alternative business references, as he did for the ads.

<u>Front cover headline:</u>

Professionally written sales materials – *at the ready.*

<u>Inside 2-page spread:</u>

Ever find yourself stuck for words?

Writing your own sales and advertising materials is a time-consuming business – but how else can you attract new [pupils] [members] and tell them about your [services] [facilities]?

By having Goode words at the ready.

Now you can put your message across with style and originality, without paying the earth for the privilege.

- Compelling letters
- Hard-hitting mailshots
- Intriguing advertising
- Persuasive handouts

How does the service work?

Goode words at the ready is an exciting new concept created by an experienced copywriter and [qualified driving instructor] [golfing enthusiast].

It offers you immediate access to professionally written and designed promotional materials at a fraction of the cost of using agencies. You can select from a range of ready-to-use letters, leaflets and advertisements, all of which can be personalised to your business.

Prices from only £xx

Goode words at the ready gives you the flexibility to choose the items you need and can afford, in any combination that suits you best. A leaflet handout describing your [services] [facilities], for example, would cost you just £xx.

All the items are written from first-hand experience so you can be confident they speak your language.

Prefer a more individual approach? No problem.

An alternative option is available on a fee-per-project basis, with materials written to your specific requirements. This service also includes newsletters and press releases for added value and immediacy. There's no charge for the initial brief and prices are agreed on the spot – and kept to.

Want to know more?

Goode words at the ready is available now. It could make a big difference to your profile – and your profits.

For details, call Andrew Goode now on

01234 567891

Any questions? Just turn the page . . .

<u>Back cover:</u>

Goode words at the ready.
Your questions answered . . .

Q: Will I be expected to buy a minimum number of items?

A: Not at all. You can buy a single letter or a complete sales and marketing pack. The choice is yours.

Q: Can you really write with authority about a specialised business area like ours?

A: I am a [qualified ADI] [golfing management consultant], so you can have every confidence in my expertise.

Q: If I opt for your bespoke literature option, will I have the final word?

A: Every time. You will have full control throughout the writing, design and print process.

. . . can we get together?

Call Andrew Goode on 01234 567891

Spreading the word: press releases

Andrew is confident he can write a good press release to support his advertising and inserts because of the articles he has already had published. He uses the 'six honest serving-men' principle to structure his copy:

- Who? [the name behind the news]
- What? [the news itself]
- Why? [the background]
- How? [the practicalities]
- When? [availability]
- Where? [contact name and number]

145

4 January 2000

FOR IMMEDIATE RELEASE – *Better Driving Today* magazine

Local writer launches 'Goode words' business initiative

Andrew Goode, a qualified ADI and experienced business writer, is launching an exciting new service designed to help driving schools attract more business.

The *Goode words at the ready* initiative puts the emphasis on professionally written, affordably priced sales and marketing materials which can be personalised to your business. Andrew has created the service specifically for the driving school market, based on first-hand working knowledge of why – and where – these materials are most needed.

Said Andrew: 'Driving tuition is a demanding profession, often leaving little time or energy for business promotions. All too often, pupil numbers drop and schools are left with little choice than to scramble out expensive, hastily worded advertisements in the hope of a response.

'*Goode words at the ready* solves this problem by providing a range of ready-to-use letters, leaflets, press advertisements and pupil handouts. And because they are professionally written, they will enhance the profile of your school as well as increasing the flow of pupils.'

Available individually or as an integrated sales pack

Businesses have the option of selecting from a range of standardised written items, or they can choose a 'bespoke' service with materials written and designed to their specific brief.

Prices start from as little as £xx. For further information, call Andrew on 01234 567891 any time.

– ENDS –

Press enquiries to: Andrew Goode, Anystreet, Anytown, AB12 3CD. Tel/Fax: 01234 567891

Andrew writes an alternative version for the golfing trade press, just as he did for the advertising and inserts.

Making it personal: mailshots

Andrew has been doing his homework and knows that the most important element in a mailshot is the letter. This is his opportunity to talk one-to-one with his target audience, using information he has gathered over the phone.

To keep costs – and time – to a minimum, he wants to accompany the letter with a simple leaflet enclosure based on the copy he has already written for the insert. But instead of the 4-page A5 format, he folds the paper a different way to create a 6-page roll fold. The headline on the insert is more appropriate for the letter than the leaflet, so he looks for a different approach. Perhaps he could bring in the 'driving' word-link?

**How to give your business new drive
. . . with Goode words at the ready**

The roll fold format is perfect for splitting the headline between the front cover and inside fold-out page to turn it into a teaser. Andrew rearranges the insert copy slightly and his mailshot leaflet is ready. Now for the letter. He starts with the Greenlawns Golf Club, having already spoken to the membership secretary and been encouraged by the response.

**Professionally written sales materials
for Greenlawns . . . at the ready**

Dear Mr. Eagle,

It was a pleasure talking to you today and I'm delighted to write with further details of my 'Goode word' member recruitment initiative.

Goode words at the ready is a unique service developed specifically for prestigious courses like Greenlawns. As you can see from the enclosed leaflet, it places a range of professional advertising and sales materials at your disposal for a remarkably low cost.

The secret lies in the flexible and convenient format of the service. All the materials are written and designed to the highest standards – but because they are available 'off the shelf' they cost a fraction of the price you would normally pay an agency.

An understanding approach to your members

As a golfing management consultant, I know the importance of projecting the right image to club members.

You can be confident that every 'Goode word' item lives up to its name – in language and tone of voice.

I will leave you to read through the enclosed information leaflet, which I am sure you will want to discuss with your colleagues. To save you the trouble of contacting me, I will call again in a few days to arrange a mutually convenient day and time for us to meet. However, if you have any questions in the meantime, please call me on 01234 567891, daytime or evening.

Yours sincerely,

Andrew Goode

P.S. The enclosed leaflet also gives details of a valuable 'bespoke' literature option, written to your specific brief, which includes member newsletters, press releases and brochures.

Andrew's mailshot is almost complete. He turns his attention to the envelope. Should he add a message to increase the interest factor? 'Open up to new members', perhaps? He decides against it. The mailshot is following up a friendly telephone conversation and a message might detract from the personal nature of his response.

Delivering the news: door drops

Now for the final task: hand-delivered leaflets. Andrew feels these are more appropriate for small independent driving schools than golf courses. He checks Yellow Pages for the highest concentration of schools and instructors so that he can deliver the leaflets in one 'hit' and save petrol costs.

Having targeted his area, all Andrew needs are the leaflets. He has already discussed these with Maria and they both feel the format should be as simple as possible. Settling on a two-sided A5 design, Andrew turns once more to the insert copy for inspiration. A cut down version will serve his needs admirably.

Are you stuck for words?

Want to attract new pupils but haven't got time to write press ads and leaflets?

Goode words at the ready is the answer

Choose from a range of ready-to-use materials – including:

- Compelling letters
- Hard-hitting mailshots
- Intriguing advertising
- Persuasive handouts

All written by a qualified ADI who speaks your language.

Prices from only £xx

Goode words at the ready is designed for small businesses. It combines quality and flexibility with value and choice.

Ready to know more?

Simple. Just give me a call, any time, and I'll fit in with your diary.

Andrew Goode ADI

01234 567891

By including his Approved Driving Instructor (ADI) status on the leaflet, Andrew will inspire confidence in his target audience.

The campaign is launched. Is it a success?

Of course.

Further inspiration

To the best of my knowledge and belief, this is the only book dedicated to the vast potential for freelance copywriting.

If it has whetted your appetite and you want to know more about the techniques – especially those that I haven't covered such as TV and radio advertising – I recommend Alastair Crompton's superb book, *The Craft of Copywriting* (Century Business Books Limited). It was first published back in 1979 and the second edition is in its tenth reprint as I write. The book is targeted primarily at agency-based copywriters and focuses on press, poster, TV and radio advertising techniques. It is a fascinating insight into the world of big-budget advertising, packed with tips and illustrated with real campaigns throughout.

My other recommendation may surprise you (and please you, since it's free). It is Royal Mail's excellent bit-part series, *The Complete Guide to Advertising Your Business by Post*. As the title suggests, the series is aimed at small businesses and focuses, understandably, on the benefits of using mailshots as an advertising medium. But it is beautifully written and packed with information. You are given a free ring-binder to hold the various sections (which arrive every two months or so) and the entire pack is produced to a very high quality. It also takes a plain English approach to the subject, with clear signposting to help you cherry pick the information. Aunt AIDA, bless her, is very much in evidence, although she seems to have acquired a middle name – Conviction – which makes the acronym somewhat unwieldy.

You may come across other books and reference sources that have equal merit. These just happen to be the two that impressed me most.

Writers are lucky people. We get to do a job that life would be unthinkable without. And some of us are paid rather well for it. Inspired? Well don't just sit there reading a book . . . you have a campaign to launch! May all your concepts be headline events and every project a prize.

Index

CPSIA information can be obtained at www.ICGtesting.com
Printed in the USA
LVOW11s2013020816

498775LV00001B/48/P